"The term 'influencer' often refers to some celebrity-wannabe on any social media platform. It's time to burst that bubble! Jason's book provides clear examples of how to have REAL influence, something that connects and is meaningful. Don't be a falling star. Be a rising star."

—JEFFREY HAYZLETT, PRIMETIME TV & PODCAST HOST, SPEAKER,
AUTHOR, AND PART-TIME COWBOY

"*Winfluence* is one of those rare books that has practical, how-to advice, while also providing a broader, more strategic context. Learn why influencer marketing is passé and why leaders must replace it with influence marketing, or as Falls declares, *Winfluence*. Get a fresh marketing perspective on how to drive lasting brand value by getting this book for you and your team."

—CHARLENE LI, *NEW YORK TIMES* BESTSELLING AUTHOR OF *THE DISRUPTION
MINDSET*, FOUNDER AND SENIOR FELLOW AT ALTIMETER, A PROPHET COMPANY

"The expertise inside *Winfluence* is worth 100 times what the book costs. Eventually, influence marketing will be the only marketing that works, and this is the must-have handbook that teaches marketers precisely how to do it (and do it right)."

—JAY BAER, FOUNDER OF CONVINCE & CONVERT AND
COAUTHOR OF *TALK TRIGGERS*

"Jason Falls has outdone himself with *Winfluence*. Marketing leaders should read this book now because it teaches us how to do 'influence marketing' the right way. It is so easy to get caught up with just Instagrammers and YouTubers, but Jason challenges the status quo and encourages us to build influence strategies across all online channels, and offline channels, too. I love this book and so will you!"

—LISA JOY ROSNER, SENIOR VICE-PRESIDENT BRAND & DIGITAL
ORACLE CORPORATION

D0814420

"The recurring magic trick of Jason Falls and his work is that he digs into topics that are often poorly handled and makes a piece of work that becomes essential to understanding a concept. If this book weren't written by Falls, I wouldn't read it. Because it is, I trust it."

—Chris Brogan, *New York Times* bestselling author, *Trust Agents*

"I wish I could share with you how impactful, insightful, and actionable this book truly is, but words simply won't do justice. This is one that you MUST read on your own. This book will change your focus from the noun to the verb; influence instead of influencer.
A worthy investment."

—Rani Mani, head of employee advocacy, Adobe

"Influence is a verb, not a noun. Jason's fantastic new book shows you how to create a marketing strategy based on true community and real engagement, and he lays out an actionable plan for what that means in an increasingly social/digital world. *Winfluence* is the approach your business needs!"

—Ann Handley, *Wall Street Journal* bestselling author and chief content officer, MarketingProfs

"Only Jason Falls would ask a non-influencer like me to influence you to buy *Winfluence*. But when I read it, I understood it's the influence, not the influencer that is important. Jason taught me social media as we together reversed the then-declining sales of Cafepress and grew it like a weed. *Winfluence* is my graduate-level education.
It will be for you, too."

—Bob Marino, CEO, ThankYouBack and former CEO, CafePress

"Jason Falls is a marketing genius and an all-around great guy. I loved reading this book. Jason and I share many of the same philosophies and it's never been a better time to be an influence marketer!"

—Jo Ann Herold, CMO, The Honey Baked Ham Co.

"This book can simultaneously lead us to humanistic and responsible practices in today's cluttered landscape of messages and media. It is my hope that this book pushes us from a nascent idea of influence as an action and away from wasting resources on distracting approaches."

—Emily Kirkpatrick, executive director,
National Council of Teachers of English (NCTE)

"Whether you are arguing for budget increases to invest in this space or navigating the pitfalls of influencer outreach, the guidance in this book arms even the seasoned marketer with new insights and tactics for effective campaigns. Aside from Jason Falls' notoriety and expertise in the social media realm, his thoughtful examples and easy-to-digest strategies are impactful and distinctive. This is the ultimate handbook of how to do it . . . right."

—Wendy Treinen, director of brand and product communications,
GE Appliances, a Haier company

"Falls correctly pinpoints that 'influencers' are just the beginning of a much larger game of influence marketing; a game that is determining the success or failure of every brand and business."

—Erik Qualman, five-time bestselling author; *Socialnomics, Digital Leader, What Happens in Vegas Stays on YouTube*

"Falls correctly pinpoints that 'influencers' are just the beginning of a much larger game of influence marketing; a game that is determining the success or failure of every brand and business."

—Erik Qualman, five-time bestselling author; *Socialnomics, Digital Leader, What Happens in Vegas Stays on YouTube*

"For anyone who has ever ignored the opportunity of influencer marketing because it feels fake and scammy, this book will change your mind forever and help you take your brand to the top."

—Amy Landino, founder of AmyTV and bestselling author of
Good Morning, Good Life and *Vlog Like a Boss*

"As traditional advertising continues to decline, influencer marketing is on the rise and Jason gives a practical guide with a powerful step-by-step approach on making it work for your brand."

—Lewis Howes, *New York Times* bestselling author, *The School of Greatness*

"Finally, a book that combines influencer marketing with the strategy that actually makes it work. If you work in sales—and we all, in some way, work in sales—this book should be at the top of your reading list."

— Laura Gassner Otting, bestselling author of *Limitless—How to Ignore Everybody, Carve Your Own Path and Live Your Best Life*

WINFLUENCE

— reframing —

INFLUENCER MARKETING

to ignite your brand

jason falls

Entrepreneur Press®

Entrepreneur Press, Publisher
Cover Design: Andrew Welyczko
Production and Composition: Eliot House Productions

This publication is designed to provide accurate and authoritative information
in regard to the subject matter covered. It is sold with the understanding that the
publisher is not engaged in rendering legal, accounting, or other professional services.
If legal advice or other expert assistance is required, the services of a competent
professional person should be sought.

Entrepreneur Press® is a registered trademark of Entrepreneur Media, Inc.

An application to register this book for cataloging has been submitted to the Library
of Congress.

ISBN 978-1-64201-134-0 (paperback) | ISBN 978-1-61308-447-2 (ebook)

Printed in the United States of America

25 24 23 22 21   10 9 8 7 6 5 4 3 2 1

Dedication

To my mother, Sara George, the most impactful influencer of them all.

CONTENTS

— part 1 —
THE PROBLEM WITH "INFLUENCER" MARKETING

chapter 6

HOW TO BUILD INFLUENCE MARKETING CAMPAIGNS. 73

chapter 7

IDENTIFYING THOSE WITH INFLUENCE 87

chapter 8

BUILDING A CONTENT ARSENAL 107

— part IV —
THE HUMAN SIDE OF INFLUENCE

chapter 16

FOREWORD BY DAVID MEERMAN SCOTT

As I write this, it's the middle of the pandemic and I have been going through serious travel withdrawal. I've visited 107 countries, all seven continents, and all 50 states over a lifetime of travel. Under normal circumstances I've got as many as a dozen journeys booked to look forward to each year. However, by playing it Covid safe and not getting on an airplane for eight months, my stay-at-home life feels strangely incomplete.

So last month I bought a tricked-out 4x4 Mercedes Sprinter camper van so I can do some self-contained travel. With solar and diesel power plus a 21-gallon water tank feeding a small kitchen, toilet, and shower, I can live off grid for a week.

Prior to my big purchase, I never would have learned about camper vans if it hadn't been for several people in my network—those people who influence me—who were talking about them. That led me to a private group on Facebook that I joined, and for a few months I read every post about the sort of camper van that I by then had become obsessed with. I paid attention to what the more experienced people had to say, and they influenced my decision to buy a camper van of my own.

However, as I was doing my research, I also encountered people in the Facebook group who represented brands or who appeared to be paid influencers. Most of their posts felt like a sales pitch, so I dismissed them. And based on the very few numbers of comments on these posts, so did others in the group.

There is no doubt that without the influence of the people I encountered in the camper van Facebook group, I never would have purchased one of my own. I was influenced!

Celebrity spokespeople have been around for decades. In the 1950s, before he entered politics and was elected Governor of California and President of the United States, then-actor Ronald Reagan for many years was the host of General Electric Theater, a popular weekly TV show. People felt they could trust him, and sales of GE products enjoyed success as a result.

Fast forward to today and add the super-easy ability to create content via social media and, all of a sudden, many people influence others. Companies are obviously eager to tap into those people who have influence over the buyers of a particular type of product or service or who are popular with a particular group of people and build marketing programs that will attract them.

But how to do that?

Well, you can just pay up. Many companies invest a lot of money on celebrities who become paid spokespeople for their brands, frequently through posts by the celebrity on social media. However, paying hundreds of thousands of dollars to have one of the Kardashians wear a piece of jewelry to an event and posting a photo of the evening on social feeds isn't likely to lead to sustained sales if she isn't perceived as a true fan of the product.

Or you can find an up-and-coming influencer who charges way less than the Kardashians who will happily shill your product on their Instagram, complete with duck face, peace sign, and a fabulous background filled with palm trees and a swimming pool.

There is a better way! What you really should do instead is listen to my buddy Jason tell you about what he cleverly calls *Winfluence*.

I met Jason on social media more than a decade ago. At that time, Jason and I were both "snoopers" (a concept you will learn about in these pages) and we supported each other's forays into the world of social media marketing. I've followed Jason's work since then and when he told me about this book, I was eager to dig in.

This is no academic tome. Jason tells wonderful and sometimes funny stories of success (and failure). My favorite is the goat with hundreds of thousands of followers. When a farm animal has become an influencer, the online world might be weirder than you thought.

Jason also shares details on how to reach out to people effectively. I wish the hundreds of people who contact me in an average month would read this book. It's amazing how many people want me to share their products and services with my several hundred thousand followers and have no clue about how to effectively reach out to me. Most of the pitches I receive are awful. Jason will tell you what people are doing wrong as they conduct outreach and how you can get it right.

There is no doubt that the best people to champion your ideas or products are those who are the most believable, like those in the camper van Facebook group who were simply sharing their honest experiences.

Here's to your success,

—David Meerman Scott
Marketing strategist, entrepreneur, and *Wall Street Journal* bestselling author of 12 books including *Fanocracy*
www.DavidMeermanScott.com
@dmscott

THE INFLUENCER STUNT THAT WASN'T

The first of nine posts in a carousel of Instagram pictures showed her smiling, her sandy blond hair cascading over a bare shoulder, her overalls undone on one side. The wide, open-mouthed grin and half-closed eyes were tilted up as the sun shone down on an expression of sheer joy.

One arm was holding a white helmet in her lap. The other propped her up as she leaned against the seat of her 1980s-era BMW R80 motorcycle. Tiffany

Mitchell looked as happy as a woman could be, out for an afternoon ride with her friends Lindsey and Martin.

Ironically, it was her words, breaking through the image-first distraction of the world's most popular photo-sharing site, that drew the audience in. They were a shocking juxtaposition to the model of happiness before them.

"This is me and my bike about an hour before I got into an accident," they began.

No one could resist flipping through the rest of the pictures after that introduction. But there was something unsettling about the photos of the accident. They were good. They were too good. Perfect lighting, excellent color balance, incredible capture of emotion.

In one, Mitchell lay on her side, hand on head, eyes closed, her helmet in the foreground. Martin knelt beside her, reaching under her head to hold and comfort her. The sense of drama was palpable.

In another picture, Mitchell was in the same position, but the camera was closer, just a few feet away. Martin was looking off to the side as if to talk to someone. Someone had gotten her some water since the previous photo was taken.

But the Smartwater bottle is conspicuously placed, logo forward, between the helmet on the side of the pavement in the foreground and Mitchell's limp body just beyond.

Professional-grade photographs? A seemingly obvious product placement smack dab in the middle of the drama? It's easy to see why some reactions to the post were skeptical and others were outraged.

You see, Tiffany Mitchell's friend Lindsey Grace Whiddon, who took the photos in question, is a professional photographer who often snaps magazine covers of Nashville's elite. Mitchell's Instagram account (@Tifforelie), where all this went down, has about 200,000 followers. Tifforelie is an influencer. And that bottle of water rained down a shitstorm of controversy not just on her, but on influencers everywhere.

THE PERFECT STORM

Mitchell's post, which went up on Instagram in August 2019, was picked up by *BuzzFeed*, which quickly published the most incendiary comments.

BuzzFeed updated the story more than once with statements from both Mitchell and Smartwater that they did not have a working relationship and the post was not an advertisement.

In the fast-moving world of social media, though, it was too late. Mitchell was being lambasted for everything from overacting to poor ethics. The story made its way to *Cosmopolitan, Elle,* and even Britain's *The Evening Standard,* each new post pouring gasoline on the fire. *Harper's Bazaar*'s coverage of the controversy appeared under the headline, "Does the case of the influencer motorbike accident signal the death of Instagrammers?"

The same week Mitchell's story exploded across the internet, travel influencer Tupi Saravia (@Tupisaravia) was busted for photoshopping identical clouds into many of her posted images. She didn't help the influencer cause much by telling *BuzzFeed,* "I really don't see the big deal [here]."

Then actress Nicole Arbour posted a video to her 2.6 million Facebook fans accusing fellow influencer Jay Shetty of plagiarism. Shetty's motivational and inspiration content had landed him appearances on *Ellen* and *The Today Show,* along with 25 million Facebook followers, 2.9 million YouTube subscribers, and 4.7 million fans on Instagram. Arbour's video showed a dozen or more of his motivational quotes and then exposed their original sources.

The perfect storm was brewing for everyone to start bursting the influencer bubble. The skeptics were pushing the stereotype that influencers have lots of fans but little substance. One brand manager told me that when he thought of influencers, he thought of "douchebags on Instagram posting a never-ending stream of airbrushed selfies of them in some expensive outfit flashing a peace sign and sticking out pouty lips."

He added, "Why anyone would follow that narcissistic nonsense is beyond me."

Honestly, he wasn't (and isn't) far from the truth about some influencers. For every one who is genuinely productive and useful to their audience and can move the needle for some brands, there are probably two or three who fit the duck face, peace sign stereotype.

But as your parents or grandparents probably told you, when troubled times come calling, remember: "This too shall pass."

That same brand manager increased his influencer budget by 200 percent the following fiscal year. He acknowledged it will likely go up next year, too.

THE TRUTH

The truth is Tiffany Mitchell didn't fake her motorcycle accident or exploit it for a brand partnership. She posted a long series of videos explaining it all on her Instagram Stories (which, as of this writing, you can still see in her highlights at instagram.com/tifforelie). Those videos not only recounted the accident and how the pictures happened, but also explained why it was important to her to post them.

"When my bike went down, everyone reacted immediately by pulling over, rushing to my side, making sure I was stable, and calling an ambulance," she told me weeks later. "Then we waited. A few strangers pulled over to make sure I was OK. One of them brought me a water bottle and placed it near my head so I could reach it. It was during this time, once everyone knew I was all right, that Lindsey decided to document what was happening, unbeknownst to me."

She said they were on their way home from a photo shoot when the accident happened, which is why Lindsey had her camera. "It was an intense moment for all of us," she said.

And the water bottle? It was put there by one of the people who stopped to see if she was OK. "I'm so sad everyone missed that part," she said. "Giving someone water after they've been in an accident is a standard, and genuine, act of kindness. The chances of the water logo being visible in the shot Lindsey took were high, as it's duplicated on both sides of the bottle. It's not a reach to believe that was a coincidence. That man and his friend who helped were the only other accounts I tagged in the post aside from Lindsey and Martin." Mitchell added the two good Samaritans loaded her bike into their truck and drove her home.

"The goal of the post was to share something extremely vulnerable, not to get attention or sponsorships," she explained. "It was devastating to see the heart of what I was sharing get so lost, so fast, and be met with such hatred."

The moment was intense for Mitchell because of another motorcycle accident that had happened three years before, on May 16, 2016. It involved Kappel Cloninger, her "partner in work and life," as she called him. He did not survive.

Mitchell's ordeal played out across the media, both in traditional outlets and through social media. Her alleged fabrication was held up as another reason influencer marketing is fake, faddish, and frivolous. But the truth is her audience grew, and grew closer to her, because of the human connection they feel when someone shares parts of their lives that aren't polished for the cameras, even if those events are captured by a professional photographer.

Because of this emotional connection to their audiences, influencers aren't just here to stay—they may very well be the primary marketing channel of the future for many brands. In the course of the following pages, I hope to illustrate why that is, and how you and your brand can approach influencers and influencer marketing in smart and effective ways. You can win with influence . . . or, as I like to call it, Winfluence!

DEFINING WINFLUENCE

Winfluence is a new way of approaching influencer marketing so you improve your chances of success by using influence. It is different from what we've always thought of as influencer marketing because it shifts the perspective to the action rather than the channel.

Traditional "influencer" marketing focuses on the channel, or the person you will use to communicate your message; as a result, the actual purpose of the communication often gets lost.

"Influence" marketing (without the "r") focuses on the action—the act of influencing someone. That is the purpose of using the channel, the individual with influence, for your communications. The shift in perspective is subtle, but it can drastically change the actions you take and the outcomes you are used to seeing from an "influencer" focus.

Thinking in terms of the action you are trying to produce (the influence) rather than the channel you're using to produce it (an influencer) allows you to focus on the strategic implementation of the communications. It grounds you in your goal, which better ensures you actually affect your target audience. It also removes the blinders that keep marketers from seeing opportunities for influence beyond Instagram and YouTube.

That's right! Influence marketing can happen off-line, too!

WHAT YOU CAN EXPECT FROM THIS BOOK

Winfluence: Reframing Influencer Marketing to Ignite Your Brand is not merely a checklist of tactics. There will be plenty of explanations of how to "do" influencer marketing, but all that is framed within the concept of Winfluence. Winning with influence marketing means you must apply marketing strategy to the action of influence, rather than simply spell out tactics to take with influencers.

The book is divided into four parts. Part I presents a more holistic view of the problems with "influencer marketing"—both the label and the practice. Part II digs into the strategies of influence marketing, and Part III illustrates the four main purposes of influence marketing through a series of case studies that will inspire your own ideas. We end with Part IV, in which I share my thoughts on the human side of influence marketing and the responsibility we marketers have to practice the craft responsibly.

I've spent hours interviewing, researching, re-interviewing, and parsing these ideas, and then turning them into what I hope is an informative and fun read. Through in-depth interviews and case studies, I hope to illuminate the reframing of influence and the application of influencer marketing. And I hope you'll find my approach—storytelling mixed with practical, how-to content—enjoyable.

If you want a bulleted list of how-to steps with check boxes and such, Chapter 6 is for you, but you can also come hear me talk about the book at a conference or webinar near you, or follow along with my periodic influencer marketing updates online. (These are conveniently organized for you at winfluencebook.com or in my newsletter, which you can sign up for on the site.) When I have more check-box lists ready, I'll put them there.

My hope is that these stories and ideas help you better understand influence, influencers, and the value of carving out an influence marketing practice for your business, brand, or clients—and that you will realize it's about so much more than placements or impressions or conversions. I've made a career out of building relationships with people of influence, to the point that I have a touch of influence myself. But without them, I'd never have written my first book, let alone three.

I consider some of those relationships the more important friendships in my life. Many of the influencers I know have been to my house, and I've been to theirs. We know each other's children.

I'm not friends with every influencer I know, of course. Sometimes they want to keep the relationship strictly professional, and that's perfectly fine. But I'm not in it for short-term gains. I want to benefit from their audience over time, but I want them to benefit from the relationship as well.

That is what influence and influence marketing should be—a long-term investment in relationships that provides value to you and them. Influencers are, on one hand, the channel of the day. And on the other, they are your business partners, and perhaps your friends, of the future.

—Jason Falls, June 1, 2020

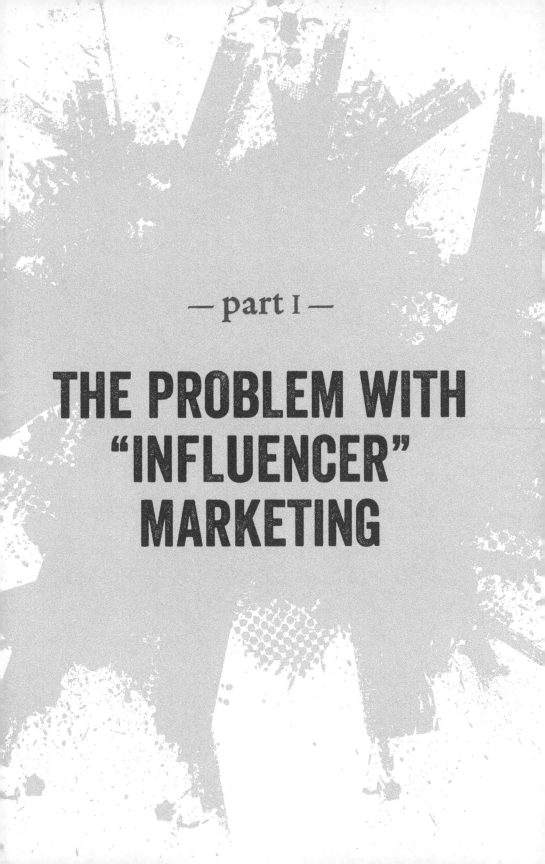

— part I —

THE PROBLEM WITH "INFLUENCER" MARKETING

HOW INFLUENCER MARKETING BECAME A PROBLEM

Billy's mom drags him around town taking pictures and videos of him, seemingly just to post them on social media sites. She dresses him up in ridiculous outfits and makes him wear sunglasses. He sits in an old lady's lap at a nursing home. He poses by a pool at a nighttime party. Not long ago, his mom made him host an evening in a dance club, complete with his picture on the flier.

Billy doesn't seem to mind. But then, he hasn't even had his first birthday yet.

Now you may be thinking Billy's mother is neglectful, even selfish, capitalizing on a child's cuteness to gain social media followers. And yes, Billy is a kid. But he's not the kind of kid you're thinking of.

Billy is a goat. As in the animal. His "mom" is owner Jo'Lee Shine. Billy goes by @realbillygotti online, and he's been dubbed "The most stylish goat in cyberspace." He has amassed 182,000 followers on Instagram to go with his 151,000 fans on Facebook. He's been a guest on *The Maury Povich Show.*

To give Real Billy Gotti some context, 182,000 is more than twice as many copies printed each day than the *Raleigh News & Observer,* one of the main daily newspapers serving Billy's home state of North Carolina. It's also larger than the circulations of papers in Tampa Bay, Cleveland, Boston, and Detroit.

Add his Facebook audience to the total. If Billy's 333,000 total fans were a publishing audience, his social media presence would rank as the 11th largest newspaper in America, just behind Houston's *Chronicle* and above Philadelphia's *Enquirer.*

Did I mention this is for a goat?

Now, I have to admit that goats give me the heebie-jeebies. Some people think they're cute or funny, but they're the demons of my nightmares. It's the eyes. They have freaky eyes.

Personal phobias aside, how the hell does a goat have more than a quarter of a million followers? Ones it can potentially influence to consider, try, or buy products?

Ironically, it all started when those very consumers, who are today influenced by goats, initially grew tired of being influenced by anyone.

In this chapter, you will learn what qualifies someone as an influencer and learn how online influencers came to be. I'll walk you through the story of how social media emerged so you understand why our current media landscape is so fractured but still full of opportunity. Finally, I will demonstrate the power of online influencers and begin to connect their influence to the formidable discipline of word-of-mouth marketing.

DEFINING INFLUENCERS

But before I go further down the goat path (or any other path, for that matter), it will be helpful to agree on what makes someone an influencer. Most people assume we're talking about YouTubers and Instagrammers—people with big social media audiences, who brands want to pay to talk about their products and services online.

That's a good starting point, but it is incomplete.

The broader definition of an influencer is anyone who has influence over another person. In a marketing context, that means anyone who might sway your decision to purchase a product or service. That could be someone with a big online audience, but it could also be your neighbor, an aunt or uncle, the barkeeper at your favorite watering hole, or even a couple of strangers in line at the DMV you overhear talking about their experience with a company or product.

For the social media influencer, I believe the role requires the *intent* to influence. But if we were to only focus on YouTubers and Instagrammers, we would be leaving out other wonderful paths to influence audiences in ways that benefit our brand. And including those is a key ingredient to Winfluence, as opposed to influence.

So for the purposes of this book, and the subsequent conversations and ideas that will come from it, my definition of an influencer is this:

> — An influencer is anyone who can persuade
> an audience to think or act differently. —

For most of this book, you can assume we're talking about individuals with mostly online audiences who have some degree of intent to build a bigger audience and monetize their impact by partnering with brands.

But as you will see in Chapters 3 and 4, I'll also make a case for reframing how we think about influence and influencers altogether. So we will talk about off-line influence as well. Or even those who create influence accidentally, with no intention of persuading people to buy.

And we'll talk about how you as a brand, business, or marketer can leverage all the different types of influencers strategically. That approach is another key ingredient that distinguishes Winfluence from influencer marketing.

HOW INFLUENCERS CAME TO BE

In the 1970s, the world was in some ways idyllic. OK, maybe the fashion trends didn't exactly have staying power. And some '70s music makes people cringe even today. But it was a simpler time.

Like most people in the U.S. in the 1970s, I grew up with four TV stations—ABC, CBS, NBC, and PBS—along with one or two country and pop radio stations, a local newspaper, a major daily newspaper that occasionally covered the news where I lived, and two or three magazines that my family subscribed to. Along with the local movie theater, a rare trip to the nearby larger city to see a live theatrical production, and some records or eight-track tapes, that was the extent of my media landscape.

To become a member of that media, you had to go to school and learn how to be a writer, director, producer, or editor: learning to uncover facts, corroborate them, and report them fairly. For broadcast media, you had to be licensed by the FCC. In print journalism, you had at least one, if not several, layers of editors, proofreaders, and fact checkers to make damn sure you didn't publish something inaccurate, incendiary, or misleading.

Ethics was also a huge part of your training. You understood that "advertorials" were pushing the boundaries of right vs. wrong, and they never, never, never came from the editorial side of the building. They weren't stories; they were ads.

Being a member of the media took time, training, and technique. And even though we didn't call them by that name, they were influencers.

Now think of news sources we turn to today. Those TV and radio stations from the 1970s still exist, but now there are also hundreds of cable TV channels, four or five local TV stations that may or may not be affiliates of the main networks, and dozens of on-demand platforms like Netflix, Hulu, Amazon Prime Video, and more.

And don't forget online video platforms like YouTube, Facebook Watch, and IGTV!

You also have a multitude of local radio stations, satellite radio, and hundreds of podcasts from which to choose. Then there are social networks, where content from all those news sources (and more) is shared. Some people rely solely on Twitter, Facebook, LinkedIn, Instagram, or Snapchat to get their friend-filtered "news" of the day.

Many news media outlets have corresponding websites that function just like newspapers, magazines, TV, or radio stations on the internet. Then there are more than 31 million blogs out there that often pose as news sites. And let's not forget social news or news aggregator sites like Reddit and Fark.

What happened?

Social media happened. The world went from a trickle of information to a flood of biblical proportions, filling every eye and ear with news, opinions, rants, and arguments from every angle and perspective imaginable.

And this flood of floods began at the turn of the century. Yes—the 21st century.

THE GENESIS OF SOCIAL MEDIA

If your mind is still ambling lazily down that small-town road in 1975, fast-forward to 2000. Beyond the Y2K bug freaking everyone out, the turn of the century was marked by a consumer revolution in technology. There was no one big, dramatic event that sparked it. Instead, consumers insisted on a series of gradual, intentional, and methodical changes that, in aggregate, turned the media landscape upside down.

First, the internet emerged as a place to explore. After the home computing market matured in the 1980s, the 1990s introduced higher-performance machines with ever-increasing processor speed and functionality. Modems for connecting to the web became standard features.

According to U.S. Census figures, the percent of American consumers with computers in the home rose from roughly 20 percent in 1990 to half of all households in 2000. Just a year later, half of all those computers had access to the internet.

Part of the reason consumers were so attracted to this new medium was their revulsion at how marketers had turned all the other mediums into spam factories.

Think I'm wrong? Let's look at the tea leaves of that era:

* Cable TV networks, which went from 28 in 1980 to 79 in 1990, continued their explosive growth rate heading toward the 21st century, with 171 in existence by 1998. Several of those networks were subscription-based, like HBO and Showtime, which allowed consumers to see long-form programming without being interrupted by ads.
* The first TiVo DVR shipped in 1999, ushering in the era of on-demand TV (no VCR needed). One of its chief appeals to consumers was the ability to skip commercials.
* Satellite radio's era began with the launch of Sirius's first satellite in July 2000. Future merger partner XM launched its first satellite nine months later. The promise both services first sold to consumers: no commercial interruptions in their music.
* Most major web browsers added the ability to block pop-up ads in the early 2000s.
* The Do Not Call Implementation Act, which established the National Do Not Call Registry, was passed by the U.S. Congress in 2003 to protect consumers from annoying and unwanted phone calls from telemarketers.
* That same year, Congress also passed the CAN-SPAM Act, an attempt to protect consumer email inboxes from the same type of intrusion.

It's kind of obvious, isn't it? Is there any other brief span in history during which so many innovations centered on stopping marketing? By the way, do you know what SPAM means, at least in the official regulatory record of the U.S. government? Brace yourself.

"CAN-SPAM" stands for Controlling the Assault of Non-Solicited Pornography *and Marketing*. There we are, standing beside pornographers as the repugnant cretins of the consumer's world.

The general distaste for advertising was perfectly addressed, Martin Luther-style, in the seminal work of the day, *The Cluetrain Manifesto* by Rick Levine, Christopher Locke, Doc Searls, and David Weinberger. This modern-day "95 Theses" was originally posted online in 1999. You can still read them all in just a few minutes at Cluetrain.com. The book version was published in 2000.

While I'm admittedly paraphrasing, these declarations said, in essence, "Stop bugging us, you marketing turds!"

The only reason this wasn't the prevailing theme of the early 21st century was the other big thing that happened around that time: Internet-based companies were multiplying like bunnies, but they forgot to develop revenue-based business models. They were thus staring down the barrel of an unstable stock market and rising interest rates. The dot-com bubble was bursting.

What does that have to do with social media? Here's my theory:

* All those internet nerds suddenly lost their companies and jobs and had to move back into their parents' basements.
* They all met online in chatrooms and forums to figure out what to do next.
* They collectively agreed that the solution to getting their jobs back was to make the internet easier to use so it would appeal to more people.
* Someone said, "Let's democratize the media and make everyone a publisher!"

OK, that last one is a stretch. I don't think changing the media landscape was *that* intentional. But the end result was certainly the same.

To be fair, we should recognize that the foundation for social media was laid prior to the dot-com bust. McKinsey & Co. said as early as 1997 that new technologies to make the world a more connected place would soon hit the market. And lest we forget, the original social media—online discussion forums, or BBSs—have been around since the low-tech 1970s. Even today these often look and feel the same as they did 20 years ago. But, cart or horse, the lowering of the barrier to entry through new technologies to make the internet more user-friendly was a critical step toward the everyone's-a-publisher world of today's social media.

Blogger was the first significant platform to emerge, debuting in August 1999. By filling out a web form much like typing in the subject line and body copy of an email, anyone could publish not just a single web page but an entire website, with as many pages as you wanted to create.

While other blogging platforms were around, like Open Diary and LiveJournal, Blogger exploded rapidly. In 2003 it was acquired by Google. Other sites followed suit in fairly rapid succession. The open-source online encyclopedia Wikipedia launched in 2001. LinkedIn launched in 2003.

It was perhaps Friendster that moved the technology to the precipice of allowing everyone to be the media. It launched in 2003 and reached millions of users in just weeks. The big selling point? The site not only included the ability to not only add friends and send them either public or private messages but also to publish blogs and other types of content in a stream, wall, or feed for your fans or followers to see.

Friendster users were the first to be given a full set of publishing tools to circumvent traditional print and even photojournalists' work. When Myspace launched in 2003 with similar publishing mechanisms and added more bells and whistles, with image, audio, and even video functionality, it poured gasoline on the Friendster fire. In three short years, Myspace surpassed Google to become the most visited website in the world, albeit briefly.

In 2004, Flickr brought photography publishing to the masses. That same year saw the launch of both Facebook and WordPress, a Blogger killer that today drives approximately one-third of all websites in the world. YouTube launched in 2005.

It can be argued that all these technologies were children of the dot-com bust of 2000. Perhaps I'm romanticizing the emergence of social media a bit, but the quest to lower that barrier to entry was complete in just a few short years. By 2005, anyone with an internet connection could write, photograph, record, or film their own content and put it online for the world to see.

The downside is that most of them did just that.

THE SIGNAL TO NOISE PROBLEM

Social media, perhaps more than any other creation, perfectly underlines the idea that just because you *can* do something doesn't mean you *should*.

I don't mean that social media shouldn't have been created. I mean that while anyone can be a publisher, I think we can all agree that not everyone should be.

Mind you, this isn't a personal political statement. I'm sometimes as annoyed at peace signs and duck faces as I am about hate speech and fake news posts. But the lowering of that technology barrier seems to have opened a Pandora's box.

Unlike the 1970s, we don't just have four TV channels and a handful of newspapers seeking to entertain us. The internet has also given us websites like YouTube and Instagram, which compete for our attention. Within those websites, there are millions of channels—specific users' content feeds—also vying for our eyeballs.

The vast majority of that content and those channels is, frankly, crap. Almost 70 percent of Instagram users have fewer than 1,000 followers, and the average user has just 150. Most of Instagram is just a sea of noise.

But where there is noise, signal will always emerge—an anomaly that stands out in the noise, like looking down on a busy sidewalk and spotting a red umbrella in a sea of black ones. In the world of social media content, that signal is quality content, art, opinions, ideas, and more, generated by people who have a knack for engaging with and building an audience.

The biggest difference between the influencers who have emerged as relevant in social media today and the Dan Rathers, Ryan Seacrests, or Nora Ephrons of yesterday's traditional media is formal training. Certainly those three and many other old-school journalists and entertainers have talent. But so does Perez Hilton.

The everyone-is-a-publisher era ushered in a time when people who were interested in a topic could share their knowledge and thoughts about it. Struggling authors, perhaps denied by editors and turned away by publishing companies, could now self-publish and build their own audiences without traditional marketing support.

Take J.C. Hutchins. His *7th Son* trilogy concept was rejected by dozens of literary agents before he elected to begin recording the story and publishing it via podcasts in the mid-2000s. By the time his episodes reached the second in the three-volume series of novels, he had amassed more than 20,000 listeners. Hutchins eventually hit more than 50,000 listeners, and the podcast crossed the 1 million downloads milestone. St. Martin's Press has since published two of his books. One of them wasn't even a *7th Son* title.

Dane Cook is well-known for leveraging Myspace to build his stand-up comedy career. While he already had an established career before he launched his page in 2003, it helped him go from a struggling featured act to a multimillion-dollar headliner. Cook's clever trolling of online chatrooms to gauge audience interests and brilliant use of exclusive ticket promotions on Myspace resulted in sold-out shows without the need for six-figure advertising budgets.

Whether it was podcasts, Myspace, YouTube, blogs, Twitter, or the later sites Facebook and Instagram, talented content producers used these alternate pathways to build their own audiences.

Today, you don't have to work the system to score a celebrity chef TV show. You can just film yourself cooking or write down your recipes and put them on a website, a YouTube channel, or a Facebook post. Certainly many people will try this and attract little to no attention. But those with the right combination of personality, style, unique content, and promotional smarts succeed.

Those who have attracted audiences online this way are social media influencers. They may only appeal to people who enjoy their content but don't necessarily trust them for product recommendations. But they may have their audience waiting with bated breath for the next suggestion to go out and buy or try. We'll talk more about the difference between influencers and those with influence in Chapter 3.

The problem for you, in the end, is how to tell the signal from the noise. Are these untrained bumps in the soil actually diamonds in the rough? To know the answer, we simply have to ask the people we want to sell to.

INFLUENCERS ARE LEGIT

I can hear you skeptics in the back thinking it: "Influencers, schminfluencers. Nobody actually pays attention to these people. And those peace signs and duck lips don't equate to business metrics like sales or revenue."

You're not just wrong. You're damn wrong.

Rakuten Marketing surveyed 3,600 shoppers from around the world in early 2019 to find out exactly how much impact these new media icons really have. Almost two-thirds of those surveyed (61 percent) interact with an online influencer at least once per day. More than one-third (35 percent) interact with them multiple times per day. And some 32 percent of those surveyed admitted to shopping online daily while almost half (48 percent) will browse or buy online every week.

But here's the important part: Consumers admitted to discovering at least one new brand or product weekly *from an online influencer*. And if that wasn't enough to convince you these types of influencers should be your new best friends, 87 percent of those surveyed said they were inspired to make a purchase based on what they saw from an influencer online.

Let's be real: If someone told you that a branded blimp flying over a football stadium inspired 87 percent of the people in the stadium to make a purchase from that company, you would funnel all your marketing dollars into buying as many blimps as you could get your hands on. The consumer behavior is there. Social media influencers are affecting it. What more proof do you need?

Well, you need to know how well the specific influencers you work with can convert. And we'll talk more about how that happens later. But you also need to understand how online influencers can affect branding and awareness, website traffic, search engine results, and even issues management.

To do that, you need to understand what influencer marketing really is, in terms everyone can understand. When your company gives an influencer something to share about its products, services, or even positions on issues, and the influencer tells their audience about it, that is word-of-mouth marketing. Influencers are the online manifestation of word-of-mouth marketing, or WOMM for short.

Andy Sernovitz's bestselling and groundbreaking 2006 book *Word of Mouth Marketing: How Smart Companies Get People Talking* laid out the power of WOMM nicely. Word-of-mouth marketing drives sales as much as five times more than paid advertising impressions and 200 times higher consideration than from ads. (Sernovitz's book is now in its fourth edition, with the latest revision published in 2015.)

An Engagement Labs study in 2017 revealed that 19 percent of a given brand's sales are directly impacted by people talking about it, while 40 percent are influenced by WOM. Jay Baer and Daniel Lemin's 2018 "Chatter Matters" research, a companion to their bestselling book *Talk Triggers: The Complete Guide to Creating Customers with Word of Mouth*, moved the needle even further.

Its data, derived from surveys of 1,001 randomly selected U.S. consumers, showed that word of mouth is directly responsible for 19 percent of all purchases and impacts as much as 90 percent of them. "Chatter Matters" research also found that aside from personal experience and familiarity with brands, the most important and trusted factors driving a consumer's purchases were, in order: recommendations from family and friends, online reviews, and expert reviews.

Those experts reviewing products? Online influencers. Reviews? Many of them are posted by influencers and can be part of your influencer marketing efforts. Recommendations from family and friends? They're influencers, too. They may not have 250,000 Twitter followers, but they're influential nonetheless.

On the B2B side of the aisle, influencers are increasingly vital to a brand's success. According to research firm Gartner, 83 percent of an enterprise buyer's journey is spent studying what is being said in the industry about the products, as opposed to talking to product reps.

Where do you think they're doing that studying? Gartner's 2020 B2B buying journey report shows that more than one-fourth of their studying time (27 percent) is done online, where they search, read industry blogs, scan industry forums and message boards, and connect with experts (read: influencers) in the subject matters served by the products. Another 18 percent of their time is spent researching off-line, and 22 percent is spent discussing purchases with a buying group. What are those groups full of? Fellow shoppers who have done the same type of online research. Oh, and perhaps some influencers, too.

Influencer Marketing Hub surveyed more than 800 agencies, brands, and relevant professionals in the influencer marketing world in 2019 and found that 92 percent agreed that influencer marketing is an effective marketing channel. The same survey revealed that 80 percent are either budgeting the same or devoting more to influencer marketing in the 12 months following the survey. The percent planning to increase their budget? Sixty-three.

WORD OF MOUTH AS INFLUENCER MARKETING

Word-of-mouth marketing capitalizes on a person's willingness to tell others about a product or service. It engages any audience—customers, media, influencers, employees, vendors—with information, education, entertainment, or even tangible objects and goods that inspire them to go tell someone else in turn.

It aligns with a content principle I've talked about for the better part of the past decade: Your job as a marketer is to create content that makes an audience say, "Holy smokes! That's [insert adjective here]!" If your content does that, you've struck an emotional chord and forced your audience to want to share that content.

WOMM is just that. Your content is the message you want people to share. You need to do something for your influencers, with your influencers, or perhaps give something to your influencers that makes them want to do the same thing themselves. They will then do something for or with their audience, or give their audience something that is so outstanding their audience then has to tell someone about it. If you're smart, that will include a recommendation or referral to you.

Influencer marketing is, then, a version of word-of-mouth marketing. It's what I call the manufactured starting point. You are paying someone, or providing them with some value, to start the word-of-mouth fire. Often your influencer marketing relationships will be paid partnerships. In that scenario, WOMM purists will say it's not quite word of mouth. But many of their programs begin with mavens, influencers, or paid promotions to seed the message. They may not admit it, but influence marketing is part of their approach, too. And it has been all along.

The goal of influencer marketing is to have your influencers spark that fire that becomes great word of mouth. If their followers tell friends and those people tell more friends, and you coordinate those sparks with enough of the right influencers, you get a pretty nice word of mouth *and* influencer marketing case study.

Consumers are listening—not to your press release or clever ad campaign, but to people they identify with, who earn their attention day in and day out as they bounce around the social web. These like-minded people are influencers who, when called upon, can persuade consumers to know, like, and trust your company. And when that happens, your needle will move a lot easier.

So going back to Billy at the beginning of the chapter, how does a goat have influence? It has influence because a bunch of smart people got laid off in 2000, wanted to move back out of their parents' basement, and decided to build a better web. They opened the door to the democratization of media and tore down age-old barriers between people and the power of mass communication.

They thus empowered a new generation of content providers, opinion makers, and entertainers. Including the ones who know there are plenty of people out there who don't get the heebie-jeebies from freaky-eyed goats.

WHY CONSUMERS CARE ABOUT INFLUENCERS

What do you think of when you hear the word "pudding"? For most people, it probably brings up some childhood memory of afterschool snacks (or, unfortunately, Bill Cosby commercials). But one group of people who may have a very different answer is women who love their curly hair.

Pantene Pro V Curl Defining Pudding is a popular finishing touch item in the brand's Gold Series of haircare products. It helps curly hair stay moisturized, retaining its natural curl without frizzing. According to several dozen product reviews I read, it also smells good and leaves hair shiny.

The Curl Defining Pudding was often mentioned by influencers in Pantene's Gold Series campaign in the early summer months of 2019. The Procter & Gamble brand chose 25 Black women who were Instagram influencers, with content centered on beauty, hair, and lifestyle. Four of the influencers had a good number, but not millions, of subscribers on YouTube. Each was engaged to place at least one sponsored post apiece on each channel.

The goal was to drive awareness of Pantene's Gold Series Collection, which includes the Curl Defining Pudding. At the time of the campaign, the online influencers' audiences ranged from Chizi Duru's (@chiziduru) 122,000 Instagram followers to Lisa-Jean Francois' (@lisaalamode) 36,000. (Duru also had 381,000 YouTube subscribers, which were enough to place her on both lists of Pantene Gold Series influencers—Instagram and YouTube.) In total, the potential reach of the influencer effort based on their number of followers was more than 2.5 million people.

The proof is indeed in the pudding. The posts registered 250,000 views on Instagram, earning more than 56,000 likes and 1,600 comments. The overall engagement rate of the program, according to Mediakix.com, was 12.26 percent—an outstanding ratio of engagements to reach.

On YouTube, the influencers produced 287,000 views with more than 1,000 comments and an engagement rate of about 4.5 percent. Not bad for a platform not always known for driving comments and interactions.

These numbers are strong, if not outstanding. More important for the brand, the main talking points and unique selling propositions were called out by each of the influencers. The specific products in the line, including the Curl Defining Pudding, were mentioned. The fact that the Gold Series was developed by a team of Black scientists was prominent in many of the posts. The influencer campaign did exactly what the brand team hoped to accomplish: create greater awareness of the Gold Series Collection within the intended target audience.

This was a Winfluence campaign, not just an influencer marketing one. It leveraged online influencers, but in a targeted manner with strategic purpose that moved the business forward. It wasn't just buying sponsored posts on famous Instagrammers' accounts and hoping people would think you were cool by association.

Another factor that makes this a Winfluence campaign is its construction. Even the largest advertiser in the world—Procter & Gamble—with its bleeding-edge marketing approaches, didn't spend marketing dollars on mega-influencers with millions of followers. It focused on midtier and even smaller influencers with engaged audiences who could persuade those fans to take action.

Procter & Gamble reported a 5 percent growth in organic sales from its products in fiscal 2019. Sales of the Pantene Gold Series contributed to that growth.

The world's largest advertiser turning to influencers to drive success would seem to reinforce our earlier assertion that influence marketing works. In the rest of this chapter, you'll see plenty of data to back that up. I'll also explain the concept of surrogation, which answers the question of why consumers care about what influencers have to say. You'll then understand how influence marketing connects to one of the most important types of online content for brands: ratings and reviews.

FISH WHERE THE FISH ARE

So let's take a look at *why* Procter & Gamble is investing their considerable resources in influence marketing online.

They're doing it because the internet is where consumers decide to buy products. People who buy hair-care products don't watch TV commercials, look for an ad in the Sunday paper, or flip through magazines anymore. Instead, they're looking for information online.

And more than any other company in the world, P&G knows to fish where the fish are.

The *Columbia Journalism Review* summed up the main reason consumers flock to influencers in today's media world. In a survey conducted for the *CJR* by Reuters/Ipsos in December 2019, confidence in the press was compared to mainstay institutions like the military, law enforcement, universities, the Supreme Court, Congress, and the executive branch of the U.S. government. The least trusted of those institutions? The press. The survey also revealed that about 40 percent of people get most of their news from online and social media; the same percentage get most of their news from TV. Perhaps more shocking, 60 percent of the 4,200 Americans polled believe that reporters sometimes or often get paid by their sources to write stories.

CJR's 2019 data follows a long trend in consumers' deteriorating trust in the media. A September 2018 Gallup poll found that 69 percent of U.S. adults say their trust in the news media has decreased in the past decade. In fact, between 2003 and 2016, the percentage of Americans who said they truly trusted the media fell from 54 percent to 32 percent.

Ipsos' July 2019 "Trust in the Media" report found something more specific: 46 percent of consumers around the world say they do not have much trust in traditional media, meaning newspapers, magazines, TV, and radio. Further, the 2019 Edelman Trust Barometer revealed that 74 percent of consumers across eight major countries intentionally avoid advertising. Thirty-nine percent said they had found ways to avoid almost all ads.

People don't trust traditional media. And people demand trust.

For several years now, the Edelman Trust Barometer has been the bible on understanding consumer trust. And the special report on brands may as well have been a big, flashing neon sign that said, "Consumers Trust Influencers!" In it, 63 percent of people said they trust influencers' opinions of products "much more" than what brands say about themselves. And 58 percent—almost six out of ten consumers—confirmed they had bought a new product in the past six months because of an influencer's recommendation.

Read that again. Not because of a recommendation from a family member, a friend, or an online review. More than half of people *globally* have bought something in the past six months based on the recommendation of an online influencer.

Consumers also confirm another assertion we've discussed: It's not always about popularity. An influencer's ability to connect with them in a meaningful way is a better indicator of persuasive success than how many followers they have or how famous they are.

Edelman's namesake president and CEO, Richard Edelman, told *Ad Age* while discussing the report, "Influencers matter. They're credible."

To be fair, Edelman's 2019 "Global Report" also showed conflicting levels of trust in media, reporting that 64 percent of people globally trust traditional media, rising to 65 percent in the United States. Social media, on the other hand, is generally not as trusted, with only 44 percent globally and 34 percent in the U.S. claiming it as a trustworthy resource.

As an institution, however, "media" broadly scores a 47 on Edelman's Trust Barometer around the world, meaning that 53 percent of people globally don't trust it. In the U.S., that number falls slightly to 52 percent.

CONFLICTING PERSPECTIVES

Advertising agency UM also conducts an annual survey of consumers that asks about influencers, but its "Wave 9 Study" in 2019 revealed an opposing view. Only 4 percent of the 56,000 consumers it surveyed around the world said they believe information that comes from influencers. Only 8 percent believe information shared on social media sites.

The poll showed, for example, that only 36 percent of people in Britain trust influencer opinions on products and services. Globally, trust for their opinions was a bit higher, at 42 percent.

What on earth can explain the disparity between these two surveys?

Simply put, the statistics here are answers to different questions that don't necessarily have anything to do with each other. The UM data seems to answer the questions "Do you believe what you see on social media is true?" and "Do you believe the information you learn from influencers?" The Edelman data seems to answer, "Do you trust what an influencer says more or less than you trust what a brand says?"

My go-to resource for gut-checking research data, Edison Research senior vice president Tom Webster, admitted there's no way to truly compare the data without closely analyzing the original research. He did say, however, that he would not put these studies up against each other. "It's a false equivalency," he said.

It shouldn't be lost on us that for every anomaly in the research reports we find, we discover three or four counterpoints from either consumers or brands. Estée Lauder CEO Fabrizio Freda surprised the media, if not his shareholders, on the company's fourth-quarter earnings call in August 2019.

"Over time we have invested much more in advertising, and now I would say that every one of our brands has some investment depending on where they are," he reported. "These investments are mainly now in digital. Seventy-five percent of our investments now are in digital social media influencers, and they're revealing to be highly productive."

Freda went on to explain that influencers help Estée Lauder reach targeted audiences so the company can focus its spending and attention where there is growth. He credited influencers with giving his brands a "better rate of return" on advertising spend.

The numbers presented during Freda's shareholder call? Net sales in Q2 of $14.86 billion. That was a 9 percent increase from the year before— while spending 75 percent of its ad budget on influencers!

Major corporations are also using technology to capitalize on influencers in ways far beyond just YouTube and Instagram. Deirdre Paul and Christopher Volinsky of AT&T Labs Research hold a patent for a method and "apparatus" to identify influencers within a social network. For example, if a company has a list of customers, the patent would help them identify the social networks those customers belong to and figure out which people on their customers' networks are influencers. The patent points out that the ability to identify influential individuals in the network, the ones who are good at affecting how others purchase products or services, is important for marketing.

The patent was first applied for in 2007. It was granted in 2018.

WORD OF THE DAY: SURROGATION

The indicators are there. So is the data. Consumers give a damn about influencers. Enlightened brands know this and give a damn about them, too. And while we've presented a valid reason for this—that traditional media is less trusted, or at least less consumed—there is a still more compelling answer to the question "Why?"

The concept of *surrogation*—using other people's experiences as a guide to your own behavior—is the psychological trigger behind everything from online reviews to the seemingly ubiquitous commercial tag line "Four out of five dentists surveyed recommend . . ." which was Trident chewing gum's slogan in the 1970s.

Surrogation is why review sites like Yelp or Angie's List are successful. Consumers don't necessarily have direct experience with restaurants, hotels, plumbers, or other businesses, so they need to use other people's experiences before they decide where to spend their money.

Like review sites, which help us quickly narrow in on a decision to buy (or not), online influencers act as a surrogate for our own experience. I would argue that they are better surrogates in many ways than the random reviewers on sites like Yelp, because consumers who allow influencer surrogation to affect their thinking generally have already been following those influencers. There's some compelling reason for that.

It could be that the influencer is informative or entertaining. It could be the consumer thinks their worldviews are similar and wants their social media feeds to reinforce that worldview. It might be that the consumer aspires to be like that influencer, or even that a friend recommended their content and the consumer tends to follow the friend's social cues.

Whatever the reason, consumers are more apt to allow surrogation with influencers because they feel as if they know them. That can rarely be said for people who leave reviews on Amazon or OpenTable or even a highly reliable review site like Common Sense Media.

Whether through reading reviews or taking recommendations from influencers, surrogation happens more frequently today because of the increasing array of options for our attention and corresponding shrinkage of time. And influencers are relevant authorities people accept as surrogates more readily than others.

In Robert Cialdini's seminal 1984 book *Influence: The Psychology of Persuasion*, he explained that in the "rush of modern life," it is easy to forget to distinguish between relevant authorities and irrelevant authorities. There are two ways to incorporate that analysis into your thinking about influencer marketing.

The first is that it explains what we're saying here: People are too inundated with information and activities and too pressed for time to analyze who they get advice from. Older consumers have begun to distrust the traditional media and opinion makers. Younger consumers never trusted them in the first place.

Thus, people are hungry for influencers to help them make quick decisions about products, services, events, destinations, movies, and more. They can connect with someone with 250,000 fans who posts a lot of content about style and fashion and, over time, trust that their recommendation for the latest offering from Dolce & Gabbana or Maybelline is worth buying.

The other way to incorporate Cialdini's thoughts on distinguishing between relevant and irrelevant authorities is something he called the six principles of persuasion, which we'll cover in more detail in the next chapter.

Is surrogation a reliable way to make decisions? Does this psychological solution to our busy-ness problem mean influencer marketing can get into our head and make us behave differently than we otherwise would?

Daniel Gilbert, a psychologist at Harvard University and author of the bestselling book *Stumbling on Happiness*, is an expert on human behavior when it comes to judgment and decision making. He talked about surrogation with Shankar Vedantam on the *Hidden Brain* podcast in September 2019.

"I'm not saying that surrogation is a perfect way to make decisions," he said on the program. "Imagination is so utterly flawed that surrogation, even with all of its problems, turns out to be a better method than that."

Baer and Lemin's "Chatter Matters" research, which we touched on in Chapter 1, laid out the priority of consumer trust for product recommendations. On the authors' seven-point scale, which you can see in Figure 2–1 on page 25, personal experience rated as the most valuable source of information, at 6.0. Brand familiarity came second at 5.5, and a recommendation from a friend or family member was third at 5.2.

Online reviews came in as the fourth most trusted source of purchase recommendations (5.0). Expert reviews, in which I would include influencers (but with a stipulation I'll explain momentarily), are fifth at 4.9. Discounts or coupons, news coverage, advertising, and posts from friends or brands on social media round out the top ten.

Clearly an online review and an expert review are neck-and-neck in terms of what consumers trust most. However, influencers were not specifically called out in this research, and Lemin clarified that the "expert reviews" were from professional reviewers, magazine reports, and similar.

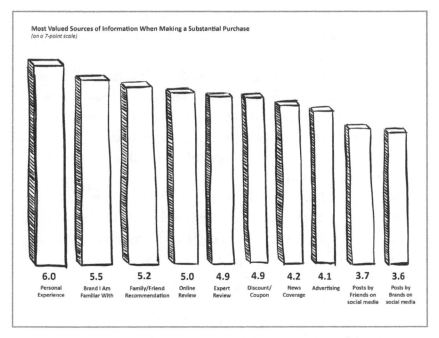

figure 2–1. Most Valued Sources of Information When Making a Substantial Purchase —"Chatter Matters: The 2018 Word of Mouth Report," Jay Baer and Daniel Lemin

They are influencers in their own right, but they are not exactly analogous to online influencers of all kinds.

Still, can we agree that influencer reviews and product recommendations can also be considered "expert" reviews? Lemin answered that question with another question.

"To some degree, it depends on how you define an 'influencer,'" he said. "You can think of an influencer as a semiprofessional expert on a topic or just someone who has a big platform—celebrities, elected officials, or athletes. The other way to look at an influencer is someone who influences purchases and decision making, and that isn't always famous people. Your friends and neighbors, for example."

After I proposed my definition of an influencer—anyone who creates content for an audience with the intention of informing, entertaining, or influencing them, he quickly agreed.

"I think professional reviewers are influencers," Lemin said. "In almost all cases they are. In their professional role, they're an influencer. I would probably lump them together."

But let's not forget that someone who follows an influencer's content—including product recommendations and reviews—is familiar with said expert. I contend that might make an expert review even more reliable and effective than a regular online review. This would mean influencers are more valued than online reviewers or even reviews from experts who are unfamiliar to the consumer.

Gilbert, the Harvard psychologist, agreed that aligns with typical human behavior. "Your hypothesis sounds reasonable to me," he said in an email. "If only because we know people are more influenced by single anecdotes than by data that aggregate many people's experiences."

Gilbert then pointed me to the Volvo example in Richard Nisbett and Lee Ross' groundbreaking 1980 work of social psychology, *Human Inference: Strategies and Shortcomings in Social Judgment.* In the Volvo example, someone is considering purchasing either a Volvo or a Saab. They consult *Consumer Reports* and see that a Volvo is mechanically superior and has a better repair record, so armed with facts and figures, they decide to buy a Volvo. Prior to making the purchase, however, they attend a party, where a friend relays a horror story of a relative's troubles with his Volvo. They now have conflicting perspectives. One is the consensus opinion of experts and reviewers, and the other is a secondhand story about the experience of a single person.

Despite a stockpile of data indicating the Volvo is the right purchase, Nisbett and Ross wrote, most people in this situation would choose a Saab. The visceral, emotional experience of the friend's story will outweigh any factual evidence to the contrary.

Their work illustrated what became known as *base rate neglect.* This happens when we are presented with information that is generally true and accepted, or at least can be understood. Then we are presented with a singular example that contradicts that generally true idea. Our minds tend to ignore the former (the base rate) in favor of the latter. One could argue it is the root problem of media consumption in American society today, but that's another book for another time.

The concept of base rate neglect supports the theory that an influencer's recommendation or review is more powerful than those of lesser-known reviewers, and it is tied to the idea of interpersonal trust. A set of headphones can have 1,329 five-star reviews on Amazon, but if Dank Dalia (@dankdalia), a Colorado-based gamer with a combined audience of over 300,000 fans across Instagram and Twitch, says they're crap, a lot of people will avoid buying them.

Conversely, if your new pruning shears have just as many one-star reviews, but Vanessa at @the.urban.farmgirl tells her 140,000-plus Instagram followers she loves them, the product will move.

Certainly unless we ask consumers specifically about the difference between influencer input and more common online reviews, we cannot know. But Lemin says it's certainly a workable hypothesis.

"Generally, everyday people—their feedback, star ratings, whatever it might be—are seen in aggregate," he agreed. "They may not have individual weight to someone going to eat at a restaurant, for example. You see someone's star rating in aggregate with hundreds of other people. But you might read a review in the newspaper or see an influencer talking about their meal at a restaurant that sways you more strongly. So yes, I think it carries extra weight. If the person has a professional role or a major following, yes. For sure."

The "Chatter Matters" research also asked where consumers typically get information about the products or services they are considering buying. While none of the responses were specifically "From online influencers," a brand's engagements with them can most certainly make the list.

The top result on that list was an online search, with 66 percent of those surveyed saying that is one way they typically get information about products they're considering buying. Influencer blog posts, YouTube videos, and even some social media posts can come up in those searches, depending on the keywords used in the query.

Websites covering a particular industry were a trusted resource for 40 percent of the people polled. Those would certainly include blogs and media sites run by influencers focused on a given industry.

As of this writing, in the fall of 2019, if you search for "eo deodorant" or "eo organic deodorant," looking for the organic deodorant made with pure essential oils, the website The Glamorganic Goddess (glamorganicgoddess. com) appears in the top ten results. The blog is run by thirtysomething breast cancer survivor Danielle Messina. Her review of EO Organic Deodorant outranks product pages on websites for Walmart, Target, and Kroger.

The final two resources for information about products or services consumers are considering buying that have relevance for influencers are rating or review websites (37 percent of respondents use) and friends on social media (22 percent). Crafty companies can engage influencers with requirements to add a rating or review on a given site for that purpose. And influencer content is often passed from friend to friend on social channels.

Consumers trust influencers for product and service information. While it may not be the most trustworthy or most frequently visited resource when people are making buying decisions, the search engines can make it so. And the presence of influencer engagement with your product or service can give your brand a halo of awareness to benefit it in social media conversations.

My assertion, then, is that the proof is indeed in the pudding. Although while Pantene Pro V Curl Defining Pudding runs about 85 cents per ounce, far cheaper than sugar-free and keto-friendly Simply Delish Natural Instant Chocolate Pudding, I still don't recommend eating it.

THE DIFFERENCE BETWEEN INFLUENCERS AND THOSE WITH INFLUENCE

Renee's craft project wasn't just going poorly. It was a miserable failure. The 18-year-old had worked hard to create something original and fun, and she had hoped it might earn her a little spending money. Despite encouragement from her friends, the project flopped. No one was interested in buying her items.

Now, if this were 1982 and Renee was writing about her frustration in notes to friends, we would all think, "Hey, you're 18 and tried to sell a craft project? That's mighty entrepreneurial of you. Keep trying. You'll land on something good one day."

But this was 2019, and Renee was writing about how frustrating it was trying to monetize a custom clothing line to capitalize on her online popularity. She didn't write about it to a couple of buddies—she wrote about it to her 2 million-plus followers on Instagram. Renee is actually Ariana Renee, known online as the fashion and style influencer Arii (@arii).

Her post flatly stated that she had sold at most 36 units of any one of her seven products and complained about the people who hadn't "kept their word" that they would buy her clothing. The total overall was 252 units sold in 13 days—not enough for the fulfillment company to actually ship the orders.

Within minutes, her followers and online commentators ripped Arii apart. She had to turn off Instagram comments to avoid seeing the never-ending flow of criticism at her expense. The popular link-sharing site Reddit featured more than one post about Arii's lament, with many tagging it as the bubble bursting on influencer marketing.

Adweek even got into the fray, sourcing quotes from professional marketers and agency types critiquing what the teenage entrepreneur did wrong.

Ironic that in an entrepreneur-driven culture, where failure in startups is often celebrated as a learning experience, we would crucify a teenager for doing just that. But in terms of influencer marketing, Arii's story did in fact illustrate a bit of a bubble. There is a large difference between an influencer and someone with actual influence.

More than 2 million people chose to allow Arii's content into their social media streams. Even an incredibly conservative estimate of someone promoting an item to 2 million-plus people would sell more than a few *thousand* units. (Two thousand units sold to a market of 2 million people is a conversion rate of 0.1 percent. That's pitiful by any channel's conversion rate standards.)

Arii is an influencer. She created consistent content over time that appealed to millions of followers. But she didn't have *influence*. She didn't engender the knowledge or feelings from her audience that would make them think, "She recommended that product. I want to buy it."

In this chapter, you will learn the difference between an influencer and someone who has influence. I'll explain the principles of persuasion and how they define that difference. You'll then see how that fundamental division created the problem Winfluence is here to solve.

What knowledge or feelings does Arii need to build in her audience to be more successful in launching a product line in the future? We can find them in the dry heat of Arizona.

THE SIX PRINCIPLES OF INFLUENCE

No one understands how an influencer can stoke the fires of an audience to get them to buy better than Robert Cialdini. We mentioned his book *Influence: The Psychology of Persuasion* in Chapter 2.

Cialdini's bestseller is based on his experiences learning, theorizing, testing, and refining persuasion in various real-world jobs over several years. He boiled that research down, along with other inputs from experts who study why we make decisions, into his 1984 masterpiece on the subject. Since then, he has written five more bestselling books on the topic of persuasion.

The framework of Cialdini's work revolves around what he calls six universal shortcuts to guiding human behavior. They are his six principles of persuasion (see Figure 3–1 on page 32). For our purposes, we'll simply assume *persuasion* and *influence* to be synonymous.

By breaking each of these down, we can begin to see how a person or brand might engender the kind of trust required to influence an audience. Let's examine Arii's case using the six principles and see if we can prescribe a smarter approach for her next product line launch.

⇄ *Reciprocity*

The first principle is easy to understand: You give to get. If Arii gives something to her audience, they want to give her something back in return. It's why when someone buys you lunch or coffee, you instinctively want to return the favor at some point.

From a marketing tactics perspective, Arii could have launched her product line with a special discount code or buy-one-get-one offer exclusively for followers (e.g., "dm me for a special code worth 10% off on

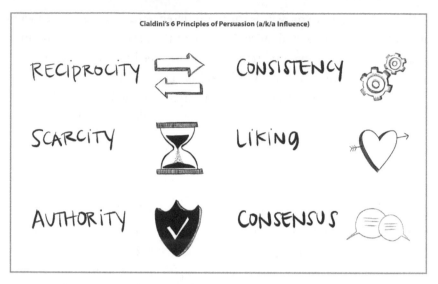

figure 3-1. Robert Cialdini's Six Principles of Persuasion

my clothing line!"). Going back even farther in her marketing timeline, she could have included fashion tips and ideas in her content over time to sow the seeds of reciprocity.

While all the content around Arii's product launch seems to have been taken down after the debacle, a quick analysis of her Instagram account shows her posing in different outfits and places, accompanied by some vague copy. But captions like "Where this flower blooms" with a couple of emojis doesn't give the audience anything useful.

Don't get me wrong. Arii's content is inspirational if you identify with her. But there isn't any advice or instruction about style or fashion along with her content. She isn't giving her followers anything besides fancy pictures of her.

A long ramp-up to the product launch with a "style tip of the day" would have at least triggered the reciprocity instinct in some members of her audience. Arii needed to give them something more if she wanted something from them in return.

⌛ Scarcity

The phrases "supplies are limited" or "for a limited time only" exist to create an aura of scarcity around the product. If we think there aren't enough for everyone, the prestige of being one of the few people to own one punches our pride and ego buttons. We have to have it!

From my understanding of Arii's product launch, it didn't include any limits on availability or time. The store was open. Buy all you like. If all of her 2 million-plus fans could shop any time, why would they rush? It would still be there tomorrow.

If, however, her product launch was "exclusive" and time-sensitive, her audience would have felt an urgency to go buy. Perhaps her first post showing her modeling her new tops could have been captioned, "I only have 1,000 of these in stock. The people who end up with these will always be my favorite fans."

For the more long-term, strategic play, Arii could have talked about the product launch for weeks in advance, consistently mentioning that only 1,000 of each item would be available. She could have priced and planned for 1,000 items to be launched each year, to make them super-exclusive. She could have influenced her audience to perceive her products as elite, hard-to-find, valuable items—and that perception would actually make them more valuable.

Much of my day-to-day work is in the spirits industry. While the world's best bourbons are typically aged eight or more years, which makes planning for product launches very difficult, distilleries have gotten smart to the scarcity game.

By choosing just a handful of barrels that have been aging longer than normal (or even longer than they should), a brand can release a special small batch of 16-, 18- or 20-year bourbon. They call it "Special Reserve" or "Distiller's Choice" and advise customers that only a few cases of this particular bourbon exist. That bottle might retail for 10 to 15 times the price of the distillery's typical offering—and on the secondary, peer-to-peer markets, it could go for 100 to 200 times the price.

People who buy a bourbon like this have absolutely zero regard or even awareness of how it tastes. They just know it's hard to find, so they want it.

Authority

This is perhaps the most important area Arii's product launch failed in. Authority is the perception or belief that you are an expert in a given subject matter. Notice I didn't say you actually *are* an expert. What matters is that your audience *thinks* you are.

If Arii wanted to build a reputation as an expert in style and fashion, she needed more than just pretty pictures of herself. She needed to position herself as an expert. By posting style and fashion tips or sharing opinions on the latest trends, she would not only look stylish but also convey her expertise about style.

As it was, Arii's content consisted mainly of images of a young woman who looks stylish. But did she *know* anything about style? Could she *teach* other people how to be stylish beyond showing them what her latest outfit looks like? It's not clear.

In all the posts I could find on Arii's Instagram account, she never even recommended a product, designer, or store to shop in. She had set no precedent for recommending purchases to others before she tried to launch her product line, so her audience did not perceive she possessed the authority to do so.

Consistency

In the context of influencer marketing, consistency is the long-term application of the previous principle of authority. Cialdini explained in his book that consistency refers to an audience's tendency to validate their previous decisions or behavior by doing something similar, even if it doesn't make much sense.

For example, if you buy Girl Scout cookies from your neighbor's daughter, and then months later her son comes by selling Boy Scout popcorn, you'll probably buy some, even if you hate popcorn. That's because you've already demonstrated the friendly behavior of supporting your neighbor's kids, and you don't want to look like an ass by saying no a second time.

For Arii's product launch, the situation is a little trickier because she didn't have products to persuade her audience to buy before then. But she could have been consistently recommending other people's products. She could even have had affiliate partnerships with various retailers or fashion brands and conditioned her audience over time to trust her product recommendations.

But if Arii really wanted to leverage the consistency principle, she could have done a monthly post where she helps raise money for a charity by asking her audience to donate money or buy a product. Then, after she establishes a baseline of charitable giving from her audience, she could launch her product line, with a certain percentage of profits going to that charity.

If her audience is used to the behavior of supporting her in a certain way, then doing it again, even on a bigger scale, is an easier sell.

♡ Liking

Would you rather buy life insurance from some random person who approaches you at a networking event or Jan, the lady from the PTA you often sit and chat with before meetings? Most people would say Jan. You like Jan. You know she at least has something in common with you, in that you send your kids to the same school.

Cialdini said, "People prefer to say yes to those that they like." This isn't a startling revelation, but it's one that influencers often overlook. While more than 2 million people technically "like" Arii, we're not just talking about clicking a button on a social network. The principle of liking is about having a positive reaction to someone.

Arii's followers probably "like" her that way, too. But don't you think they would like her better if they knew more about her? A pretty picture with a vague, emoji-riddled caption doesn't reveal much about what she likes to do, how she spends her free time, what her opinions are about various issues, or what movies and music she likes. The more Arii can share about herself, the more her audience can identify with her. They need to be able to make a strong human connection with her before they will be willing to say yes when she asks them to buy from her.

Arii can go on being liked with Instagram hearts or follow buttons if she wants to, but her product launches will go better if she tries to be liked for being Arii.

Consensus

As much as we hate to admit it, at the end of the day, we tend to be lemmings. When we think everyone else is buying this or thinking that, we tend to buy this or think that, too. It's the psychology behind "Four out of five dentists surveyed recommend!"

When we see people buying something, a switch flips in us that makes us want to buy that thing, too. It's a bit of a keeping-up-with-the-Joneses reaction, but it goes deeper than that. Cialdini explained that when hotels place signs saying "75 percent of our guests reuse their towels" and ask new guests to do so as well, towel reuse increases 26 percent.

We may buy what other people buy just because we want to look cool or keep up with our neighbors. But we are also persuaded to do things because we think we'll look bad if we don't follow the crowd. It takes extra effort to stand out and resist the flow.

Arii could create flow by partnering with influencer friends to have them wear her new products in their posts the week of her launch. She could also reinforce that other people are buying these items by sharing feedback from those who do, posting pictures of customers wearing the new designs and sharing reviews or feedback from customers.

When we create even the perception of flow, many people will fall in line.

WHY PRESCRIBE ARII'S FUTURE EFFORTS?

This is a chapter about distinguishing influencers from having influence, but it's in a book that's supposed to help *you* build influencer marketing programs. So why did I just spend so many words helping one influencer use Cialdini's principles of persuasion?

Because I wanted to show you how to better analyze the ability of influencers to persuade their audience on your behalf. We'll go further down this path in Chapter 6, but now you know how to look at an influencer's content and determine whether they are using the principles of persuasion: reciprocity, scarcity, authority, consistency, liking, and consensus.

If they are, they might be good candidates for your influencer marketing program. If not, there's a good chance they are an influencer without true influence.

A TYPOLOGY OF GERMAN-SPEAKING INFLUENCERS

Deciding whether an influencer has influence is an analytic and even academic exercise. You should challenge your own judgment of each influencer with that question as a deciding factor: Do they genuinely influence people?

You will find, however, that even if the answer is yes, there are still more things to consider and understand about your influencers. There are actually several different types of influencers, and each one can be useful for you if you understand the differences.

Florian von Wangenheim and Jana Gross, professors of technology marketing at ETH Zurich, a university in Switzerland, identified four primary types of influencers in their 2018 paper "The Big Four of Influencer Marketing—A Typology of Influencers." Studying German-speaking influencers across several social networks, they identified the categories as snoopers, informers, entertainers, and infotainers.

* *Snoopers*, the research found, consisted of what we might refer to as early adopters of social media. These are influencers who build networks of fans and followers simply because they like to show people how to use new networks. They "snoop" around a new platform, device, or technology; post lots of content about it as they learn to use it; and establish expertise on the platform, device, or technology itself.

* *Informers* are those who share their own knowledge and emerge as expert resources in a given area. These are the types of people we've referred to thus far as having true influence, rather than just being influencers. Their audience turns to them for instruction or advice.

* *Entertainers* are your celebrities or celebrity wannabes—the Ariis of the world who create entertaining and engaging content as a sort of new media performance. They don't attempt to share knowledge very often, if at all. Instead, they focus on creating attention around their lives, content, style, or hobbies.

* *Infotainers* are a hybrid of the last two types. These might be informers who have the personality or capability to make their content particularly entertaining or engaging. Or they might be entertainers who have some expertise in a given area and share that in their content.

Von Wangenheim and Gross developed what they termed an "Influencer Scheme," which plotted each type into a grid based on the breadth of an influencer's domain and the size of their social presence. A snooper has wide domain breadth (appeal) and high social presence (network engagement). Informers have narrow domain width and high social presence. Entertainers have wide domain breadth and low social presence. And infotainers have a narrow domain breadth and low social presence.

The researchers concluded that brands should focus on domain breadth and social presence more so than just reach. In other words, how they engage their audience and the persuasiveness of their content are more important than how many followers they have.

American research validates the same idea. Business professors Rakesh Mallipeddi (Tulane University), Subodha Kumar (Temple University), Chelliah Sriskandarajah (Texas A&M), and Yunxia Zhu (University of Nebraska-Lincoln) wrote in a 2018 paper, "An influencer might have a large following, but lower engagement levels, while another influencer might have a relatively lower following but higher engagement levels. As a result, selecting an influencer either by the number of followers or by engagement levels may not be optimal."

This avenue of thinking has produced the annoying, if not accurate terms *micro-influencer* and *nano-influencer*. These labels were created by agencies and influencer marketing software companies as sales gimmicks, but they were descriptive enough to catch on. While specific definitions vary, a micro-influencer is generally one who has a respectable number of followers (say, in the 2,000 to 100,000 range) but isn't famous. A nano-influencer has fewer followers than that (around 200 to 2,000) but still has influence over the ones they do have. And both are considered effective by current industry practitioners. Some people also throw in the term *mega-influencer*, referring to someone with more than 100,000 followers. Still others cap that qualification at 1 million and call anyone above that a "celebrity."

Jim Tobin, who in 2007 founded Ignite Social Media, one of the world's first social media-focused marketing firms, spun off an influencer marketing company called Carusele in 2015. He said the shift toward micro- and nano-influencers is often necessary to stay efficient.

"We look at lot at saturation rate," he explained. "What percent of an influencer's content is paid?"

Tobin relayed the story of a popular influencer whose content shifted to having more sponsored content than not. Her engagement rates dropped to the point that despite having tens of thousands of followers, she no longer had real influence.

"She called and asked why we weren't working with her anymore," Tobin recalled. "We told her, and she said, 'I understand that, but I'm getting paid every day.' I may not do it any differently if I was her, but for our clients, it's not just about reach. We want to work with influencers who get someone to click . . . to do something. That's a quality engagement."

If you listen closely, the underlying advice from both researchers and practitioners is that the size of an influencer's network or audience is secondary, if not tertiary or even irrelevant. Understanding the type of content the influencer provides, how they engage the audience they do have, and how persuasive they can be with their engagement far outweighs the number of their followers or fans.

But you must also realize that the current concept of what "influencer" marketing is has a fundamental flaw.

THE PROBLEM WITH "INFLUENCER" MARKETING

Who influences you? Consider that from a broad level. Who or what persuaded you to buy your last car? Why do you shop at one grocery store rather than another? When was the last time you tried a new restaurant, and how did you hear of it?

Most people would have a variety of answers to those questions, and it's fairly likely that none of them would be, "This woman I follow on Instagram."

My last car purchase was made after asking my Facebook connections for midsize SUV recommendations; then I consulted online consumer reviews. I shop at Kroger instead of Meijer or Walmart Neighborhood Market or the other grocery stores in Louisville, Kentucky, because my ex-wife always shopped there and found it more convenient. After we divorced, I just continued to go where she had. The last time I tried a new restaurant, it was because a co-worker recommended it.

None of these people are YouTubers or Instagrammers. I don't insist on constantly checking their Facebook Stories or latest tweets. Yet all of them have influence on me.

As we discussed in Chapter 1, online influence is an extension of word-of-mouth marketing. Since what influences us isn't limited to the online space or social networks, shouldn't we then consider "influencer" marketing the kind that leverages *anyone* who influences us?

We know there are people with big networks called "influencers" who may have an impact on our thinking or decision making when it comes to products. The marketing practitioners among you know leveraging the right online influencer can move your brand forward.

But the key word in the label isn't "online." It's "influencer."

There are many people out there with big online audiences who cannot motivate that audience to act or think differently. Arii is a perfect example. And there are people around the world with no online audience who can do everything from influencing a buying decision to starting a movement.

Greta Thunberg, the Swedish teenage environmental activist, began protesting outside Swedish parliament in August 2018, demanding that the government reduce carbon emissions. She eventually joined demonstrations in other European countries, inspired hundreds of thousands other students to "strike," and gave multiple high-profile speeches, including one at the UN Climate Action Summit that went viral online. She was named *Time* magazine's Person of the Year in 2019 and has not one but two Nobel Peace Prize nominations (2019 and 2020). At the time her activism began, she had a few dozen followers on social media.

Influencer and influence are not one and the same.

The term "influencer" should not mean someone with a big online following on social networks. It should mean someone who can influence their audience to think or act differently.

So let's rethink "influencer" marketing.

REFRAMING "INFLUENCER" MARKETING

Semantics are important. The nuances of definitions often make the difference between a trend
becoming a fad or the future.

Take blogs. The word "blog" has always been polarizing. But an organized mechanism for publishing and managing content on a website—a blog—is what fuels the pages of any newspaper or magazine site you read daily. Call them "articles" instead of "blog posts" and no one rolls their eyes.

The word "influencer" is increasingly bringing about similar eyerolls. The stereotype of the duck face/peace sign Instagrammer—someone who on the surface has developed market value based on little substance—isn't dissimilar from 2010-era attitudes about "bloggers" who seemed to gain readership by slamming brands for bad customer service.

So our re*framing* must include re*naming*.

In this chapter, I will explain that you must stop focusing on the noun (who does it) and instead consider the verb (what you're actually trying to harness). Instead of thinking about the influencer, let's think about the influence.

So from this point forward, I'll call it influence marketing. Agreed?

DEFINING INFLUENCE MARKETING

Your focal point, then, needs to be broader. If you're not just talking about influencers, in the limited sense of those with followings on social networks, who *are* you talking about?

Simply put, anyone with influence. And yes, that potentially means everyone. But as you define more context for your business or brand, plus the prospective audience you're trying to influence, you'll narrow the head count of those with influence *for you* significantly.

That brings about Winfluence.

As with any business activity, you want to approach your influence marketing strategically. The simplest definition of a strategic plan is a process to achieve a different status by accomplishing specific goals through a series of activities. The status you wish to achieve is normally higher revenue, larger market share, or improved positioning. Your goals might be to increase production, improve sales, convert competitor customers, improve or change perceptions, and so on. The specific activities could include expanding manufacturing lines, targeting a new audience segment, developing new advertising campaigns, or establishing thought leadership through PR, social media, and more.

The different status your company or brand is trying to achieve and the specific goals it will use to achieve it will likely align across all marketing executions. They certainly should if you hope to have your marketing engine working in unison to propel the company forward.

Your definition of influence marketing also needs to identify the various types of influential people at your disposal. Ed Keller and Brad Fay of marketing research firm Warc Best Practice wrote in a 2016 article, "We define influencers as everyday consumers who are substantially more likely than the average to seek out information and to share ideas, information, and recommendations with other people." Notice they didn't include "online" in their definition.

Understanding the types of people who can influence your prospective customers helps you define the various channels you can use, the goals you can accomplish with them, and the types of content you can employ. Finally, you need to look at the channels and content through a marketing filter to know what types of executions are possible.

REDEFINING THE TYPES OF INFLUENTIAL PEOPLE

By now you should have accepted that there is a distinction between an influencer and someone with influence. While you can certainly still use the term "influencer," I'll defer to "influential people," "influence partners," or "people with influence" the rest of the way to underline our reframing. We need to think differently about influence marketing, so we'll write and speak differently about it as well.

Remember, you're trying to win with influence—Winfluence—so your methodology is different than those who are just paying for sponsored Instagram posts.

To define who you would call someone with influence, just ask this question: "Who influences the audience I hope to reach?" But then you have to think about the answer from a broader perspective, and that's less simple.

Everyone is influenced by their family and friends. Many people are influenced by their boss or co-workers. Lots of people are influenced by their minister, priest, rabbi, imam, or another spiritual leader. But we are also influenced by conversations we overhear on the train or in line at the coffee shop. We are influenced by posts from friends that fly by as we thumb-scroll our way through our social media feeds. We are influenced by the movies, TV, radio, and streaming content we encounter each day.

And those are just the resources that aren't *trying* to influence us. Ads interrupt those content streams to persuade us to try or buy them instead of the competition. Billboards and signs muck up a simple drive or walk down the street, trying to sway our opinions on products, services, or politicians. Public relations and corporate communications professionals earn a living by trying to influence media coverage to affect public opinion. Then there are salespeople, both in stores and elsewhere, trying to nudge us to buy one thing or another.

It's easier to list all the types of influential people we have to choose from as a marketer by just saying, "Everyone." But that wouldn't help us figure out which ones will be most effective for our influence marketing efforts.

From a high level, the circles of influence (see Figure 4-1 below) can help you think about your impact from the perspective of your business.

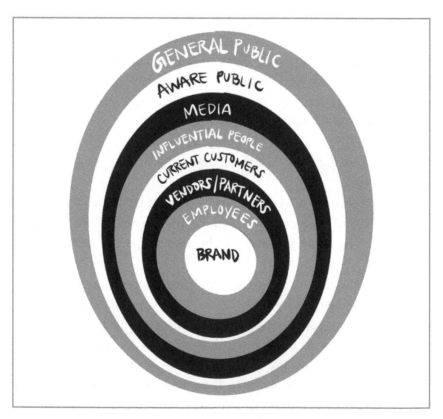

figure 4-1. The Circles of Influence

Your brand is at the center of your business's universe. The first concentric circle out from that—in other words, the first audience you try to influence about your brand—is your employees. They are easier to impact because you provide them with their livelihood. They can then influence their own family and friends to help form the core of your brand community.

The next group outward—your vendors and partners—also has a vested interest in your success. They can thus be easily influenced by you and then influence others on your behalf. Your current customers come next. They know you and your product better than anyone else because they're already using it. You can influence them through service, continued sales, and loyalty and reward programs. If you do your job well, those customers will often influence their families and friends about you.

In the next two circles, you step away from those who have already bought into your brand. Influential people and the media—who are sometimes one and the same, but they are separated here to prevent traditional PR people from having a stroke—are the bridge between your brand and the last two circles: the aware public and the general public beyond. While the previous circles can certainly influence the public for you, influential people and the media can help you connect, both directly and indirectly, to far more people at once.

Influence through the media may consist of old-school tactics like purchasing and placing advertising. It may also be via PR or media relations, where journalists can be given information or arguments to support the messages you wish to communicate to the public or other stakeholder groups.

But the circle you are probably less familiar with is that of the influential people. Yes, these can be online influencers who are very similar to the media—content providers who publish regularly and have built an audience you wish to reach. But they can also be everything from government lobbyists to perfect strangers on the street.

THE THREE TYPES OF PEOPLE WHO INFLUENCE

In my experience, the average Joe or Jane Consumer breaks down who they are influenced by into three main buckets:

1. People they know
2. People who are like them
3. People who are trying to convince them

The "people they know" group includes family, friends, co-workers, neighbors, and anyone else they identify with in their personal and professional life. These are individuals they have a real-world relationship with and trust intimately. I don't know my mayor or Oprah personally. They belong in the next group.

"People who are like them" can mean they live in the same town; are similar in age, gender, or another demographic; or share a common trait like supporting a certain sports team, musician, or even product. This group can also apply to celebrities, politicians, media members, or other notable individuals they identify with. The trust factor here derives from their sense of identity. They might trust a product recommendation or news, opinions, or ideas they share, but they wouldn't necessarily invite these people to dinner.

"People who are trying to convince them" includes anyone who doesn't belong in the first two groups and is trying to sell, persuade, convince, or otherwise influence them. Trust is hard to come by here. In fact, I would argue that if a consumer develops trust in someone from this group, that person or entity automatically moves into the second group.

This is where your business starts from when approaching prospective customers. The trick, then, is to move into one of the first two groups. That's a rudimentary explanation of what influence marketing is all about.

Let's assume that you and your brand won't get into group one: people they know and trust intimately. You can certainly stay in group three and settle for interrupting their day to force a transaction down their throat. While advertising can certainly be effective, it is often transactional and costly. But your influence marketing focus should be to make your way to the second group: people who are like them; people they trust based on familiarity or affinity.

This is a powerful reminder that perhaps the most important step in the marketing process is to know your audience. You need to know what people, organizations, businesses, or brands they identify with, have an affinity for, and trust—and why. That knowledge will be a potent component of your success in achieving that group two status.

HOW TO ALIGN WITH PEOPLE LIKE THEM

What are the possible paths of affinity and trust? If you break down the various people, organizations, businesses, and brands consumers tend to trust, you will get a sense of where to find your people with influence.

Just as you visualized circles of influence around your brand, look at your target consumers and their circles of trust. Look back at Figure 2-1 in Chapter 2, the Most Valued Sources of Information When Making a Substantial Purchase from the "Chatter Matters: The 2018 Word of Mouth Report." While this is not a survey of consumer trust, it certainly points to several touchpoints they refer to when shopping for certain types of products.

If you look at the chart through this filter, it ranks the following resources as most trusted:

1. Yourself
2. Brands you are familiar with
3. Friends and family
4. Online reviews
5. Expert reviews
6. Discounts or coupons
7. The media
8. Advertisements
9. Friends' posts in social media
10. Brands' posts in social media

But again, the chart is derived from a question about who people trust for advice and insight when making significant purchases. The Edelman Trust Barometer is biased toward looking at the trust in employers and brands. What we want to understand is who or what resources consumers trust *in general*.

My hypothesis is that a consumer's circle of trust looks like what you see in Figure 4–2 on page 48.

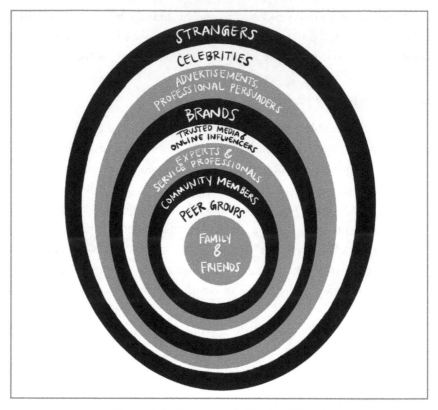

figure 4-2. Consumer's Circle of Trust

We all start with our family and friends. We trust them for product recommendations, but we also trust them to babysit our children. Next we have peer groups. This might be our classmates at school, the people in our bridge club, or even fellow members of a professional LinkedIn or Facebook Group. They have earned our trust over time through conversations and connections.

The next circle out is community members. That could be someone who lives in the same town—you know them, or you know of them—but it could also be fellow professionals in your industry whom you may have met at trade shows or conferences. These people share a set of experiences or values, so they have valuable advice for you.

Next come experts and service professionals. This includes your doctor, lawyer, accountant, thought leaders in your industry, speakers at a conference, and others with a high perceived level of expertise in the topic at hand. You may not know them personally, but you respect their experience and opinion on specific matters.

Beyond subject-matter experts, you look to trusted members of the media, which I argue also includes people with online influence. Note that I'm not referring to celebrities, which have their own ring further out on our circle of trust. I'm talking about reporters, critics, reviewers, and even niche-topic entertainers, whose content we seek out to inform our lives.

So if you stumble across Gordon Ramsay cooking a recipe on TV and are influenced by that, he's more likely categorized as a celebrity. But if you proactively follow Ramsay and all his content online, he would fall more into this category of trusted media and online influencers.

This ring is also where you typically find bloggers and marketing experts trying to subdivide people with influence into smaller groups, like "micro" or "nano." But remember, with Winfluence you are looking at influence from a broader perspective, not just those who have it on social networks. Don't get caught up in the classification game.

Brands come next in the circle of trust. The goal of that term I dislike—"influencer marketing"—is usually to borrow the trust consumers have in online influencers until you can become one yourself. However, many brands have already earned their customers' trust through great customer service, solid products, or engaging and useful content, so I've given them a ring of their own.

Consumers trust some brands, but they have a harder time trusting the next level: advertisements and what I call "professional persuaders." Professional persuaders are salesmen, government lobbyists, affiliate marketers, and similar individuals whose only job is to persuade you to buy some product or idea. They are not interested in you as anything other than a potential customer.

Celebrities fall outside this ring simply because you wouldn't trust most of them for qualified opinions on product recommendations and other issues. Research on ads using celebrity spokespeople consistently shows that ads with them are less effective than ads without. Valerie O'Regan, a Cal State Fullerton political science professor who studies the impact of celebrity endorsements on politics, wrote in a 2014 paper that young adults are more apt to listen to non-celebrity individuals when deciding how to vote, for example.

Finally, the outermost ring is for strangers. Few of us would trust a stranger to watch our purse or backpack while we went to the bathroom in a restaurant, but we might choose to try KFC's new concoction on their recommendation.

This underlines an important stipulation about the consumer's circle of trust: The circles for one person may be different for someone else. Some individuals trust celebrities far more than they trust the media, for example. Some don't trust brands at all, meaning those wouldn't even appear on their chart. And, yes, in some circumstances even our own circles change, as the stranger in front of us at the convenience store may just persuade us to buy a ticket for the Powerball that day.

The line between the media and online influencers circle and the celebrities circle can also blur, as we alluded to with the Gordon Ramsay example earlier. So remember that the circles may shift or vary, depending on the specific audience or audience member. This categorization, though, is my attempt at a general view.

Also remember these are all subcategories in the larger "People Like Them" category. These are the people who have influence over your audience. The more impact you can have closer to their inner circle of family and friends, the more effective your influence marketing efforts will be.

TYPES OF IMPACT

Before we start to layer on the marketing filter to our circles of trust, let's first look at what types of impact these people with influence can have. Influence is generally thought of as persuasion, but that's looking at the potential impact through a narrow lens.

Yes, someone in line behind you at the grocery store can influence you to buy a product by telling you they use it and like it. They've persuaded you to buy something through their influence, fueled by interpersonal cues like body language, tone of voice, or even how they dress.

But that same person can also say something about a news headline they read today that makes you think twice about a political issue or inspires you to do more research on the topic when you get home.

The four broad types of impact each of these circles of trust can have with people are:

1. Persuasion
2. Consideration
3. Exploration
4. Information

Let's look at each of them in turn.

Persuasion

Persuasion is when someone with influence convinces someone to take action. My friend Erik Deckers and I wrote about his wife Toni's persuasive skills in our book *No Bullshit Social Media: The All-Business, No-Hype Guide to Social Media Marketing*. At the time, she had maybe 150 followers on social media (this was in 2011). But she'd influenced three family members to buy Toyota RAV4s for their next vehicle. Within her family, she was a persuasive person with influence.

Consideration

When the person of influence isn't trying to ram a product or ideology down their audience's throat, they take a subtler approach to persuasion by encouraging them to consider the idea, product, or perspective. Ironically, given today's hot-button political environment, it's typically candidates that opt for this approach. They lay out their platforms and ask you to consider them when deciding who to vote for. Your best friend might also ask you to consider going to the gym with them—they would illustrate the benefits while not judging you if you decided against it.

Exploration

Similar to consideration, the impact of exploration helps an audience form an opinion by exploring a topic or idea on their own. Let's say a stranger in line mentions, "I want to recycle, but the local waste disposal company just dumps the recycled waste in with all the landfill stuff." You may ask where they heard that, but before you decide to stop recycling, you'll go home and do some investigating on your own, exploring the topic to make your own determination about how to react.

Information

And then there's the simple awareness impact of information. My daughter likes to apply her own influence on me after she learns something new in school or from the various YouTubers she likes to watch. I've learned to be ready for more than a two-sentence answer when I ask, "What did you learn in school today?" Consumers are both like my daughter and me. They want to be informed (or aware) so they can, in turn, inform their friends.

APPLY THE MARKETING FILTER

As we place the marketing filter over the circles of trust and examine the types of impact these people of influence can have, you will start to see the different types of influence we'll be looking into deeper in Chapters 10 to 14.

Businesses, brands, and organizations can use influence to drive *passion* around their product, service, or worldview. This connects the dots between people with influence and word-of-mouth marketing.

People of influence can be primed to share *experiences* with a product, service, or organization. This ties influence marketing to the all-important online activation around ratings and reviews.

Brands can leverage people of influence to build *association* between a brand and the influential person's audience, worldview, or ideas. Often done through community events, charity connections, or even media tie-ins, this sphere of influence aligns nicely with the brand's PR discipline.

Finally, in what's probably the headliner, influence can be leveraged for *persuasion*. It can move people to try, buy, attend, or vote. This is the fundamental connection between influence marketing and advertising, sales, and promotions.

Now that you've reframed influence marketing and widened your lens to take in more than just YouTubers and Instagrammers, let's run your new connection points to those prospective customers and audiences through the filter of marketing strategy. Remember:

Influence + Strategy = Winfluence.

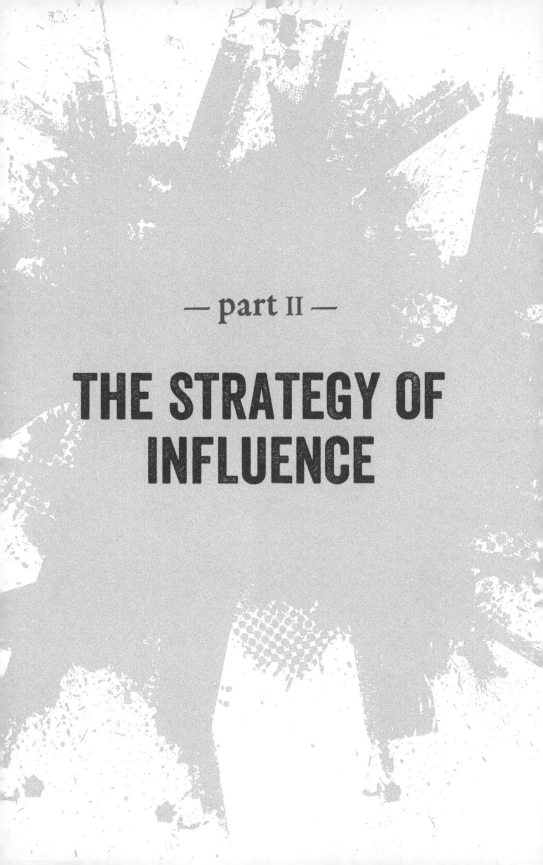

— part II —

THE STRATEGY OF INFLUENCE

APPROACHING INFLUENCE MARKETING STRATEGICALLY

Every Friday for six months, I would get a call from the CEO of a client company. (On the phone?! *I know!*) This was in the mid-2000s, as the world of social media was just breaking into the C-suite as a potential investment. He seemed concerned about the money he was spending for me to "play on the internet," as he may have put it once or twice.

His phone calls were always promptly at 9:15 A.M. He never said hello. I would just pick up the phone and hear "Jason? How many fans do we have on Facebook?"

Never mind that he could go to the company Facebook page from his own computer and find out. What's client service if you can't humor the CEO with a quick check on your follower count each Friday, right?

So I shrugged off the intrusion and told him what he wanted to know. But it bugged me.

Why did he care so much about Facebook followers? Even back then, most of us who were building out social media strategies were preaching that it's not the number of followers that truly counts, but the quality of those followers and what you can persuade them to do. It was the seed of the thinking that separates Winfluence from influencer marketing.

In an attempt to find out why he was so obsessed, and perhaps to have someone tell him he could see his company's Facebook follower count any time he wanted, I finally asked his vice president of marketing about the calls.

"Oh, you don't know?" he laughed. "He has a standing 12 o'clock golf game with three of his buddies. None of them know a thing about social media. He likes to brag about how many Facebook fans he has to them."

Satisfied that it wasn't his skepticism but his ego that was behind the calls, I just kept answering them and giving him the new and improved number. I didn't think much more about it. Until I needed to.

As the client relationship moved into the third and then the fourth quarter, with new fiscal year budgets coming to the forefront, the CEO's fondness for Facebook followers wouldn't be enough to justify more spend. I needed to prove that social media wasn't just "playing on the internet." I needed him to start thinking about it strategically.

The next time he called, I was distracted, crunching on a Friday deadline, and flat out didn't want to look up his fan count.

"Jason?" he barked into the phone. "How many fans do we have on Facebook?"

"Honestly, I don't have time to look," I said, finally exasperated. "If you go to the Facebook page on your computer, you can see the number over on the right-hand side, just under the About section."

Perturbed, he snapped back, "You don't have time to tell me how many fans we have? Why not?!"

I took a deep breath and gave him an honest answer: "Because I'm too busy trying to figure out how to get them to buy your products!"

He was quiet for a second.

"Oh! Well, then, get back to work!" And hung up.

In this chapter, I'll dig deeper into the proper strategic approach to influence marketing. You'll learn how to assess what influence marketing can accomplish and then decide what you want it to accomplish for your brand. I'll tie the strategy together by explaining my philosophy of "planning to measure."

LADDER UP

Nothing you do in marketing should be done without laddering up. That's the term many strategists use to indicate that whatever you're doing should contribute to the overall efforts of your department, business, or brand.

A car salesperson's activity should ladder up to the sales department's goals and objectives. The sales department's goals and objectives should ladder up to the marketing department's goals and objectives. And the marketing team's activities should ladder up to the dealership's business plan, or perhaps the goals and objectives of the manufacturer's marketing and sales team.

If you have a clear understanding and explanation of how your day-to-day activities feed the goals of your department, division, and, ultimately, business, then you're executing on a strategy. You're laddering up appropriately.

Influence marketing is no different. When you lay out your goals and objectives for your relationships with people of influence, you shouldn't just make some up at random. You should use your marketing goals and objectives, which hopefully have been formulated as extensions of the business's or brand's goals and objectives, as the impetus for the who, what, when, where, and why of your influence efforts.

This is Winfluence vs. influencer marketing.

In *No Bullshit Social Media*, Erik Deckers and I laid out a strategic approach for social media marketing. We wrote that in order to approach social media strategically, you have to first know what business objectives social media can accomplish and then map those to your own business objectives. Only then can you choose the right strategic approach to social media.

You should apply the same process to influence marketing. To approach it strategically, you first have to understand what the possibilities are. What can influence marketing do for your business? From those options, you must choose what you want it to do for your business. Then you can make smart, strategic decisions on how you'll use influential people in your marketing efforts.

THE BUSINESS DRIVERS OF INFLUENCE MARKETING

Erik and I listed seven drivers of social media marketing in *No Bullshit Social Media*. They are:

1. Social media can help build branding and awareness.
2. Social media can extend your public relations.
3. Social media can help protect your reputation.
4. Social media can help build community (or audience).
5. Social media can help facilitate customer service.
6. Social media can supplement R&D.
7. Social media can drive leads or sales.

If I were to reassess these now, some nine years later, I would fold public relations into branding and awareness and reduce the list to six. But each of these drivers has some relevant connection to influence marketing. And all six (or seven) can be used to ladder up to your overall marketing and business goals.

So what would the business drivers of influence marketing be? Well, let's review the ones for social media marketing:

1. *Can influential people help you build branding and awareness?* Certainly.
2. *Can influential people extend your public relations?* Yes, but that's more of their place in the operation than a strategic goal. So let's

fold that into branding and awareness, since influential people are simply additional channels to reach audiences.

3. *Can influential people help protect your reputation?* Absolutely.
4. *Can influential people help build community or audience?* You betcha.
5. *Can influential people facilitate customer service?* While I'm sure you could argue a case for it, that's a bit of a stretch, so no.
6. *Can influential people supplement R&D?* Sure. In fact, qualified experts in your industry are incredibly useful to an R&D team.
7. *Finally, can influential people drive leads or sales?* Definitely.

People of influence are also often used for goals like increasing social media followers, email subscribers, website visitors, or even online mentions or reviews. While these are all individually important, they are tactics, not strategies.

Taking my cue from the social media strategies that have generally proved correct in the nine years since *No Bullshit Social Media* was published, I believe the business drivers of influence marketing should at minimum include these five:

1. Influential people can drive brand awareness.
2. Influential people can help protect your reputation.
3. Influential people can help build your audience or community.
4. Influential people can supplement R&D.
5. Influential people can drive leads or sales.

Is that all? Let's start at the highest level and work our way down, so we know we're laddering up. Working from the top down, think about the overall strategy or strategies for your business. You might list items like:

1. Growth (of market share, mind share, or revenue)
2. Differentiation (of product or brand)
3. Acquisition (of resources or competitors)
4. Pricing (for margin or competitive standing)

All the business drivers we've identified complement each of these in various ways. Most of them fit nicely into an overall growth strategy, especially of market share and mind share. Differentiation can also include positioning, and what better way to position a product than to have a certain type of person of influence talk about or use it?

Acquisition and pricing are a little trickier, but for many B2B companies, aligning with certain influential people can tee up successful meetings to gain funding or partnerships. PR techniques can also be used with an influential person to seed ideas that lead to conversations about mergers and acquisitions. And while it's not often discussed (but frequently practiced), PR methods can be deployed to apply public pressure to speed up or slow down big deals.

Pricing strategies may not include people of influence in the formative stages, but they can certainly be a mechanism to successfully communicate or position the product or service's new pricing.

Do you see how starting from the top down works?

If you find yourself in the position of needing to work from the bottom up, you can. It is common to get excited about an idea, start talking to an influential person about it, pitch it across the organization, and even execute it before someone says, "Does this ladder up to my strategy?"

While it's certainly a better practice to work from the top down, aligning strategies to tactics and goals to objectives, working from the bottom up is simple. Look at the tactics and executions you're working with. List the overall business goals they might accomplish (awareness, sales, community building, etc.), and then align what the execution does with what your business is trying to do. You'll generally find a common thread to build on, and sometimes the strategic filter will even make the tactical execution stronger.

Provided you work for a smart company or have smart clients, the overall business strategies have been set long before you are charged with building marketing approaches to support them. Of course, the most successful companies include the marketing leadership when they formulate the business strategy, so you may have input before you have to ladder up. Either way, you most likely have what you need to get started.

START WITH THE BUSINESS GOALS

Let's say your business's overall goal is to increase market share, which will require increasing customers and sales. Marketing can contribute to that by creating better awareness of brand and product; differentiating the brand or product from its competitors; building stronger relationships with customers, community members, media, and those with influence; and communicating direct sales opportunities and information to various stakeholders.

So you pick some combination of marketing strategies to accomplish your goals: advertising to persuade your audiences to purchase; PR efforts to associate or align your product or service with corresponding themes, people, and events; ratings and reviews to validate your offerings; and word-of-mouth or loyalty programs to drive enthusiasm for your product. Within each of these strategies, which I'll discuss further in terms of influence marketing in Part III, you choose a variety of tactics.

In that overall marketing strategy, you know that people with influence can help in multiple ways. They can serve as the benchmark for alignment or association in your PR campaign. Influential people are perhaps better than random customers when it comes to validating your offerings in ratings and reviews. You've already learned how influential people are extensions of word-of-mouth advertising and, thus, can drive enthusiasm around your brand. So you start with a strategic reason and specific goals that ladder up to your overall business.

That, in a nutshell, is approaching influence marketing strategically. That is Winfluencing. But without that ultimate sense of purpose and contribution to the overall plan, influence marketing is just a dangling participle of tactical nothing.

LET STRATEGIES GUIDE TACTICS

The tactical executions that everyone is most impressed by or proud of are the ones that start with, "Here's what we did . . ." and finish with "Here's how it ladders up to what we were trying to do . . ."

Take the spirits industry, which can be tricky to navigate. While they are self-governing through the Distilled Spirits Council of the United States, most makers of whiskey, rum, vodka, gin, tequila, and such (i.e., anything distilled after fermentation) generally must follow very specific rules.

One of those rules is that spirit brands cannot name a restaurant, bar, or store as a location where you can buy or consume their product.

Regional and local distributors are responsible for promoting the product they supply at the local level. Brands must stick to broad, high-level awareness and promotions.

In the winter of 2018–2019, however, 1792 Bourbon, a client of Cornett, the ad agency I work for, was faced with a unique challenge when two Southern California grocery stores requested the brand do something to increase sales volume in their stores. The distributor was already doing its normal rounds of promotions, so how else could 1792 Bourbon help while staying on the right side of the rules?

The request laddered up to the brand's overall objectives of growing case volume sales, particularly in a key market like SoCal. Kris Comstock, the senior brand manager for Sazerac bourbon portfolio, asked if regional influence partners could help solve the problem.

The brand turned to Barlow Gilmore, known on Instagram as @the weekendmixologist, and Hannah Chamberlain, the cocktail mistress behind @spiritedla. Both were given the same challenge and collaborated with Comstock and his team to formulate a creative but compliant approach.

Each would post cocktail recipes using 1792 Bourbon, suggesting in their posts that not only were the cocktails fit to be made at your home bar but also that the spirit was most likely available at your local grocery store. No specific location was mentioned, in accordance with the rules, but the directive was to go shopping at a grocery store, not a liquor or package goods outlet or a bar.

Chamberlain added perhaps the perfect garnish to the effort, penning a lengthy blog post with the perfect Valentine's Day food and drink recipes for her followers to make for a romantic holiday dinner-at-home date. The big payoff to the post was . . . wait for it . . . a grocery list that included a bottle of 1792 Bourbon.

Did the campaign work? While neither Sazerac nor the retailers would share specific sales data, neither was as concerned about the sales volume issue come spring. And while the influence marketing effort was clever and certainly helped meet the retailers' request, the distributor, retailer, and brand all contributed in multiple ways to drive more brand volume sales during that period.

Still, by starting with the strategy and then working through influence partners to develop tactics that ladder up to the overall goal, they met a very specific challenge.

Unfortunately, many brands and even ad agencies flip this method, focusing on tactics before they think about strategy (or without ever considering strategy at all!). It can certainly be easier to focus on creative content and projects to execute with a fun online influence partner, but just having one say they like your product, rather than giving their audience specific instructions on how to find, buy, and use it, is unlikely to be effective.

Pepsi's "Join In" flop from 2017 fits this description. The brand seemed intent on making some kind of social statement by making a video that showed celebrity influencer Kendall Jenner defusing a protest by handing a policeman a Pepsi. It was so intent on making that statement that it failed to recognize the #BlackLivesMatter and #BlueLivesMatter movements and debates online; racial tensions amplified by a seemingly racist and xenophobic president; and real protests with reports of violence that were actually happening in the U.S. The ad was widely criticized, and the company quickly pulled it and apologized.

The brand's focus on tactics in this case didn't necessarily turn it 180 degrees from strategy. Over the years, Pepsi has been consistent with messaging that it refreshes a new generation of diverse, joyful people. But the "joyful" piece is where the "Join In" ad went into an out-of-control carom. Public perception of the brand hit a ten-year low after it pulled the ad.

It is incumbent upon us, the marketers, to engage those with influence who not only understand the business of influence but the business we are in as well—at least insofar as they can understand that we must ladder up to our overall business goals. Anyone who does not understand this will not serve us well, and their analytics will not reflect the same type of progress toward our goals.

MEASURE TO YOUR GOALS

Without a doubt, the most frequently asked questions marketing thought leaders have gotten over the past 20 years have been about measurement.

Frankly, this has always baffled me. If your goal is to do X, then you measure X. You either hit it or you don't.

The disconnect is that social media, and other emerging channels of marketing communications, have often been given marching orders to achieve goals they aren't well-suited for. Until very recently, the C-suite has looked at emerging channels only through the filter of whether they drive revenue. Sometimes they can, but sometimes they're better-suited for other business objectives.

Think about it from a logical perspective. If social media is a place where you can connect with and amass an audience of people who like you, it's not a big leap to say this is a way to communicate with your existing customers. Why would someone who is unfamiliar with you or has never bought from you want to connect with you online? Your internet audience is people you already know.

Wouldn't it then be logical to use that channel as a customer service or customer retention effort? That's not to say you can't derive new revenue from this audience. Repeat purchases are typically much better than new ones because they cost less to produce.

But isn't it also logical to say that thinking of this audience of existing customers only as a revenue channel is shortsighted? I think so.

To avoid the disconnect-and-deliver measures of success that make the C-suite happy, we have to first understand the overall business strategy and goals. We then have to determine what each of our marketing channels is best-suited to accomplish (i.e., what its business drivers are). Finally, we have to choose marketing goals that a) ladder up to business goals and b) are feasible for the channel.

Measurement, then, becomes not a muddled, confusing battle with spreadsheets, application programming interfaces (APIs), and formulas. It's just about answering the question, "Did we meet our goal?" Or, more realistically, "How much closer are we to our goal now than when we started?"

PLAN TO MEASURE

Regardless of how simple or complex your measurement structures are, you have to have them in place *before you start*. That means you have to plan to measure.

Not planning to measure is like putting your family in the van, backing out to the end of the driveway, turning in your seat, and asking, "OK! Where are we going on vacation?"

You haven't packed. You don't have plane tickets. You don't have hotel reservations. You didn't get cash from the bank. You haven't asked anyone to feed the cats. How on earth do you expect to go on a vacation?

Not planning to measure is the same thing for your business. If you don't know how to capture the data you want, you'll get to the end of the campaign, effort, or fiscal year and say, "How did we do?" That's when you'll realize you don't know, and you didn't set the right data traps along the way to find out.

That does not qualify as Winfluence!

On a strategic scale, planning to measure means you have to define not just your goals, but how you will measure progress toward them as well. What metrics will answer the question "How much closer are we to our goal?" The simpler you keep the goal, the easier it will be to analyze and measure.

On a tactical scale, planning to measure means putting the right tools and benchmarks in place, setting calendars and the like to perform the function of measurement and analysis.

For your measurement strategy, you might say, "Our goal is to increase new customers from our social media channels." You'll measure that by monitoring online sales from traffic that visited your site from social channels and social media efforts. Thus, the tactical extension of planning to measure is setting up the mechanisms to do this:

* Set your website analytics to capture the specific goal instances of inbound traffic from social media networks or programs.
* Perhaps build out separate objectives for raw organic traffic vs. specific social media campaigns, paid social executions, or even influence marketing efforts focused on social channels.
* Assign Urchin Tracking Module (UTM) parameters to links given to each channel of influence, each paid social post, or any special social media execution. (UTM parameters are strings of code added to a link that allows the owner of the destination website to see more information about a visitor based on where they clicked the

link.) See "The Power of UTM Parameters" sidebar below for more specifics on UTM parameters.

* Set weekly or monthly calendar reminders to pull the sales data from your website analytics software, filter out repeat customers, and break it down by goals.
* Compare each source, medium, influence partner, and campaign, and look at volume and percentage increase or decrease to know how each is working to get you closer to your final goal.

The Power of UTM Parameters

UTM parameters are additional characters you can add to any website link or URL to enable analytics software to better identify characteristics of the traffic produced by the specific link. It's those characters you sometimes see after a question mark in a URL, like site.com/page?utm_source=jasonfalls.

By giving your people of influence specific links to use with properly coded UTM parameters, your website analytics can show you exactly what each influence partner (or source) produced in terms of visitors, conversions, and sales on your website. It can also show you how all the influence partners together (also referred to as a medium) fared against other mediums, like paid search, organic search, and the like.

Using Google's free Campaign URL Builder (https://ga-dev-tools.appspot.com/campaign-url-builder/), you can assign a specific source, a medium, a name for the campaign, and a content description.

NOTE: Take it easy on your influence partners. Once you have that big, long URL, run it through a URL shortener like Bitly (bitly.com) to make it more manageable. Bitly allows you to customize your short link, too, so you can produce something like bit.ly/fromfalls for a link you might give to me.

To some people, that list may seem very complex. And it is complex—you have to take some steps to ensure it works well. But it's not difficult. Doing it means you planned to measure, and with a few clicks and a few minutes to read, you can answer the question, "How much closer are we to our goal?"

MEASURE INFLUENTIAL PEOPLE GRANULARLY

In our example, influential individuals are one source of new customers. Your website analytics will tell you which one drove the most people to your site, and comparing the budgets you had for each will indicate which were most efficient. Comparing these mostly online influencers as a whole to other channels like paid social, organic social, or even non-social media channels will help you understand how effective influence marketing is compared with other methods of reaching new customers online.

The trick to measuring everything by individual person of influence, or even by various types of social traffic, is planning, distributing, and successfully deploying UTM parameters. Your analytics reports can show you a spreadsheet-style ranking by social network and by influential person or method—or even influential individual divided by social network—if you and your person with influence manage them well.

To illustrate this, I actually performed a little influence marketing myself. In November 2019, I reached out to my friend Chris Brogan, a longtime pal in the marketing industry. I asked him for a simple favor: post a tweet and a Facebook post using specific links I provided that would drive visitors to the Influence Marketing resource page on my website.

My test was to illustrate that we can use Google Analytics to show not only how much traffic an influential person can drive to a page but also how much they can drive from each of his networks. Thanks to our long relationship as colleagues, friends, and collaborators, Chris was happy to help. I would get a good graphic for my book, and he would get some free exposure to all of you (though with 340,000-plus followers on Twitter, he doesn't need much help) plus the satisfaction of helping a friend, which is something he thrives upon.

Figure 5–1 on page 70 shows the Google Analytics view of traffic acquisition sources to my website, filtered by source and medium. The

JasonFalls.com Traffic to Chris Brogan Social Posts									
Source/Medium	Acquisition			Behavior			Conversions	Goal 5: Resource Visits	
	Users	New Users	Sessions	Bounce Rate	Pages/ Sessions	Avg. Session Duration	Resource Visits (Goal 5 Conversion Rate)	Resource Visits (Goal 5 Completions)	Resource Visits (Goal 5 Value)
Brogan	47 % of Total 10.38% (453)	47 % of Total 10.83% (434)	58 % of Total 11.46% (506)	81.03% Avg. for view: 79.64% (1.75%)	1.29 Avg. for view: 1.27 (1.44%)	00:00:14 Avg. for view: 00:00:37 (-62.49%)	82.76% Avg. for view: 10.87% (661.38%)	48 % of Total 87.27% (55)	$0.00 % of Total 00.00% ($0.00)
Twitter Posts	9 % of Total 1.09% (453)	9 % of Total 2.07% (454)	10 % of Total 1.98% (506)	80.00% Avg. for view: 79.64% (0.45%)	0.90 Avg. for view: 1.27 (-29.40%)	00:00:14 Avg. for view: 00:00:37 (-62.84%)	90.00% Avg. for view: 10.87% (728.00%)	9 % of Total 16.36% (55)	$0.00 % of Total 00.00% ($0.00)
Facebook Posts	38 % of Total 8.39% (453)	38 % of Total 8.76% (434)	48 % of Total 9.49% (506)	81.25% Avg. for view: 79.64% (2.02%)	1.38 Avg. for view: 1.27 (7.87%)	00:00:14 Avg. for view: 00:00:37 (-62.41%)	81.25% Avg. for view: 10.87% (647.50%)	39 % of Total 70.91% (55)	$0.00 % of Total 00.00% ($0.00)
1. brogan/influence									
Brogan	47 (100.00%)	47 (100.00%)	58 (100.00%)	81.03%	1.29	00:00:14	82.76%	48 (100.00%)	$0.00 (0.00%)
Twitter Posts	9 (100.00%)	9 (100.00%)	10 (100.00%)	80.00%	0.90	00:00:14	90.00%	9 (100.00%)	$0.00 (0.00%)
Facebook Posts	38 (100.00%)	38 (100.00%)	48 (100.00%)	81.25%	1.38	00:00:14	81.25%	39 (100.00%)	$0.00 (0.00%)

figure 5–1. JasonFalls.com Traffic from Chris Brogan Social Posts, November 16, 2019

top three, larger rows show the overall traffic from Brogan (a source in my URL parameters) and a breakdown of the traffic into Twitter posts and Facebook posts.

The bottom three rows showed the same breakdown, but this time listed under Source (Brogan) and Medium (Influence), which was filtered down to just "brogan/influencers" for this view. If I had asked five or six influential people to do this experiment and given them all custom URLs with specific source designations for their channels, they would be organized here as "brogan/influence," "smith/influence," "jones/influence," "adams/influence," and so on.

You can see that 47 users came to my website from links with my URL's source parameter "Brogan." Nine came from Twitter posts and 38 from Facebook posts. You can see the new user counts, how many sessions those users produced, and their site behavior in columns 2 to 6 under acquisition and behavior. Then, for the last three columns, you can see the breakdown of Brogan traffic by his Twitter and Facebook links filtered through Goal 5 in my analytics software of visiting the Influence Marketing resource page on my website. If you're wondering how 48 of the 47 users completed the goal of going to the page, one of them came twice, probably by clicking on the link, leaving the site, and then clicking on it again.

By using this method on a larger scale with multiple influential people, we can not only track our website impact from each person with influence but we can also separate out each of their respective channels to see which ones work better. This is incredibly powerful when it comes to measuring your current success—and it's infinitely more powerful in helping you optimize around the most effective channels in the future.

Illustrating an influential individual's value to your website traffic and conversions is but one piece of the measurement pie, however. There are many things an influence partner will say and do that don't link back to your website, and many potential channels for them to say and do them on. We'll dive deeper into measuring influence marketing in Chapter 15.

Just remember that in order to approach influence marketing strategically, you cannot think about measurement after the fact. Start with your goals, plan to measure toward them, and leverage the data traps you've set in the planning process to prove the strategy worked (or didn't), or to illustrate how much closer to the overall goal you progressed.

THE RESIDUAL BENEFITS OF BEING SMART WITH INFLUENCE PARTNERS

It's also good to consider that sometimes influence marketing isn't just about intentional strategy. Michael Brito, whose resume reads like a who's who of important tech companies (Sony, Intel, Hewlett-Packard, Yahoo!) and marketing agencies (Edelman, W2O Group, Zeno Group), said Microsoft's use of influence partners over the past 10 to 15 years is something to behold, but it's not something drawn up on a whiteboard or in a strategy deck.

"Take the term 'digital transformation,'" Brito explained. "Every B2B technology company wants to be associated with it. In fact, if you go to Google and try to buy that keyword, it's like $25 a click.

"But seven, eight years ago, before the term became popular, Microsoft was doing influencer research," he continued. "They were looking at influencers and how they were talking about the shift in business with social media, technology, and integration. Microsoft picked up on these influencers that were gravitating around the idea of digital transformation."

Brito said Microsoft began partnering with those people of influence to create owned content—blog posts, white papers, webinars—around the topic. Now if you look for anything about digital transformation online, Microsoft owns a lot of real estate. And Google searches reward that.

"Whenever the media mentions digital transformation, they're talking about Microsoft ten times more than other vendors," Brito offered. "And it's because they were looking at influencers and studying behavior to incorporate what they found into their marketing. And it required no program activation whatsoever."

Microsoft was just using influence partners as a natural byproduct of knowing their market, identifying the players in the audience, and building relationships with them. Was it strategic? Certainly. Was it the intentional outcome of a written strategy and execution plan? Nope.

These organic successes are derived from strategic planning, however. Without the intention of engaging with and understanding people with influence, Microsoft would never have been able to dream up, much less coordinate, such a success. It takes intention, immersion, and consistent engagement with influence partners to see unplanned successes emerge.

The logical next step, then, in laying a foundation for those future organic successes is to build influence marketing campaigns. You have to do it to be good at it.

While I told you in the introduction I did not want this to be a step-by-step, how-to business book, we've reached the point when a blueprint for executing all this is necessary. So let's roll up our sleeves and get the how-to down.

HOW TO BUILD INFLUENCE MARKETING CAMPAIGNS

It's time to move from strategy to action, but there still remains a world of preparation. Planning influence marketing campaigns is far more than just deciding we want to use influence partners and here's the goal we're going to shoot for. People who skim the surface of preparation aren't Winfluencing. Remember that online influence partners care about *their* goals, so building offers and opportunities for them need to integrate what *they* want with what *you* want.

As clichéd as it may seem in our link-bait world, I still find lists and mnemonic devices to remember step-by-step processes useful. In Chapter 5, we reviewed the seven business drivers of social media marketing from my first book. These were the seven strategic goals Erik Deckers and I determined, from years of working with brands, that social media could provide.

So yes, I'm guilty of the occasional listicle or silly alliteration to remember things. But they work, so sue me.

Building influence marketing campaigns, in my experience and practice, boils down to six steps. So, if you'll excuse the repetition, I present you with the six steps to building influence marketing campaigns! (Try to hear a dramatic, Monty Pythonesque trumpet blast in your mind each time you read that, and the mnemonic will stick better.)

I went the extra mile to make them alliterative, for those who prefer the dork factor turned up to 11. The six steps, which are illustrated in Figure 6–1 below, are:

figure 6–1. The Six Steps to Building Influence Marketing Campaigns

1. *Decide Goals.* With Winfluence, as opposed to influencer marketing, you must begin with the end in mind. What do you really want to accomplish with your influence marketing program, and how will that ladder up to your overall marketing and business goals?

2. *Define Audiences.* Then you need to think deeply about who you want the marketing program to persuade, convince, or have an effect upon. Knowing who you're going after makes the next step far more effective.

3. *Delineate Influential People.* Next, you'll zero in on those who can truly impact the audience you're trying to reach. This prevents wasting time or resources on "look at me" online influencers who won't help your business.

4. *Develop Assets.* Now you have to give those people with influence the content they need to successfully spread your message. This means you'll need to plan, write, design, and produce content for their accounts.

5. *Deliver Messages.* The rubber meets the road as you craft messages to your chosen influence partners to recruit them to help you achieve the goal. And as you manage the execution of the program where the influence partners deliver your messages to their audiences.

6. *Determine Successes.* Finally, you'll look at the influence marketing program's analytics to determine whether it is succeeding or something more needs to be done. And don't forget: You don't wait until the end to measure. You're going to plan that upfront.

On the surface, these "Six Ds" make sense, right? But just taking those brief descriptions and running with them is like reading "add salt" to a recipe and thinking you know how to cook. You need to know how much salt to add, how the salt affects the taste, what other spices should be added to make it taste great, and so on. Now let's dive deep into each of the six steps to get our recipe for influence marketing success written down in our cookbook.

DECIDE GOALS

Goals are usually not overlooked in digital marketing and social media, but they are often confused. As we discussed in Chapter 5, there is often a C-suite disconnect on new and emerging media channels.

How many times have you worked hard to drive better engagement, increase brand mentions, or even improve customer service quality scores, only to have your CEO ask, "What was the ROI?" If your goal is better awareness, more website visitors, or higher customer service scores, ROI is the wrong question to ask.

Return on investment is an accounting metric that the C-suite is often fixated on, and understandably so. But companies invest in lots of activities that are not directly tied to a financial output. Some marketing is focused on soft metrics, too. Still, the financial question is important to the folks who sign the checks, so we have to consider it.

In no way am I arguing that digital marketing, social media, or even influence marketing should be given a revenue pass. But I am arguing that if we are going to set goals, we need to a) try to include revenue or sales metrics in them and correlate them as best we can, and b) consistently communicate those goals so that everyone, including the CEO, knows what they are and how we'll measure them.

For influence marketing programs, we're generally not focused on financial returns but on leveraging influence partners to help accomplish our marketing goals. What do those goals look like?

We came up with the five business drivers of influence marketing in Chapter 5:

1. Influential people can drive brand awareness.
2. Influential people can help protect your reputation.
3. Influential people can help build your audience or community.
4. Influential people can supplement R&D.
5. Influential people can drive direct leads or sales.

Our overall strategy will be to drive one or more of those. They filter themselves down to goals that, in turn, ladder back up to the strategy.

If your strategic purpose for using influence marketing is to drive brand awareness, your goals will be about increasing audience, spreading messaging, and the like. Some goals might be:

* Increase website visitors
* Increase social media followers
* Increase email subscribers
* Increase the reach of social content
* Generate more online buzz

If protecting your reputation is your strategic purpose, you might think of these goals:

* Improve ratings and reviews
* Increase search rankings for critical industry topics
* Increase exposure of company thought leadership content

When building audience or community, many of your awareness goals come into play, but so do other types of goals:

* Increase website visitors
* Increase social media followers
* Increase email subscribers
* Increase engagement rates on social channels
* Increase participation in loyalty or feedback groups

R&D goals are typically very focused:

* Generate new ideas from influence stakeholders
* Generate new features from influence stakeholders
* Generate new revenue from influence-sourced ideas

And when you focus your strategies on driving sales and leads, the goals are pretty simple:

* Generate revenue
* Generate sales
* Generate leads
* Drive more foot traffic in retail stores

You can set any number of marketing or communications goals—or even concrete business goals with sales or leads—for your influence marketing program. Once again, though, you must do so upfront by thinking through what goals ladder up to your overall business strategies.

In my experience, it is important to establish one goal as the primary measure of success for your campaign. You may say, "Yes, I want that!" to all the examples I've listed, but if you try to do them all with one influence marketing program or, worse, a single influential partner, you probably won't be happy with your results.

Influential people, both in comparison to each other and in comparison to other communications mechanisms like advertising or direct mail, will be effective at helping you achieve some of your goals—not all of them at once. Focusing on one goal for your influence marketing campaign will help you develop effective calls to action to achieve it.

The Call to Action

When you're determining goals for your influence marketing program, ask yourself: What should your influential person ask their audience to do? That's what you should measure as your primary goal.

If you want them to say, "Go visit the brand's website to learn more," then your goal is to drive website traffic. Perhaps a secondary measurement should be how these better-informed consumers talk about your product.

If you want them to tell their audience, "Go visit their retail stores, located in seven places around town. Look them up online," then your goal is to drive foot traffic in your retail stores. Your secondary measurement there can be the volume of local search traffic looking for your name, days after the influential person mentions the call to action.

As you zero in on your goal, consider how you will measure it. For example, it may seem impossible to measure how much traffic an influence partner drives to your retail stores. But what if you give them an exclusive coupon code to share with their audience, or instructions to mention the posts to the store clerk for a discount or special gift? Then you can use the number of coupons redeemed, and how much revenue you derived from those people, as measures to determine the value of your campaign.

You can also get deeper into your analytics and give your influence partners exclusive links to share. Adding UTM parameters to the link, which are easy and free to use, will allow each partner to appear as a source and the collection of "Influence" showing as a medium in your analytics, just like Google, Facebook, Yahoo!, and other websites. This allows you to see the impact each individual influence partner has on your website. If you track online sales, conversions, leads, and other financial metrics, you can easily determine the monetary value of each one.

Or let's say your goal is to change the way people talk about or understand a certain issue or your brand. For instance, political operatives or communications officers for government agencies try to influence how people think about or vote on specific issues. Companies may need to change perceptions about a previously faulty product or do community outreach after layoffs or closures.

Measuring public opinion may seem challenging for an influence marketing program. Traditionally, public opinion has been measured by taking polls and surveys before and after a campaign. This can still work, but the wonderful world of social media offers a far less involved option.

Social listening software allows you to gather public conversations containing a given keyword or phrase and apply sentiment analysis (as well as other types of review) to the conversation. If overall online conversation about your brand showed a 30 percent negative sentiment before your campaign and a 21 percent negative sentiment afterward, your campaign had a 9 percent net positive effect.

Figure 6–2 on page 80 shows a conversation analysis of online mentions of Dirt Devil vacuums and the use cases consumers mention for them the most. Since removing pet and other hair plus cleaning hardwood floors appear most often, perhaps you arm influence partners with these insights and a directive to push the use of the product in a college dorm. You will know success if the volume of conversation about those purposes rises at the end of your campaign.

Again, if you don't use social listening to determine your success with a behavioral or opinion goal, you'll need to survey or poll your audience

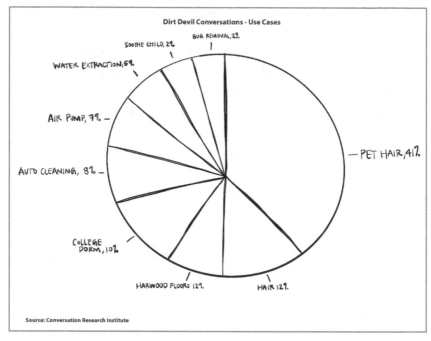

figure 6–2. Dirt Devil Conversations—Use Cases

before you begin and then again after you finish, to assign quantitative numbers to your measures.

Whether your goal is to drive website traffic, change people's opinions, or anything in between, you can also correlate those measures of success to sales and revenue. In the Dirt Devil example, you can track sales among college-aged consumers, or survey customers to ask where they intend to use their vacuum. However, this might prove tricky and even produce numbers that are not in your favor. After all, a lot of things impact sales and revenue. One influence marketing program isn't likely to emerge as the single reason for an increase in either, unless that's the only marketing you're doing.

Choosing your primary goal and determining how to measure it takes careful thinking. But that is truly the most important part of your influence marketing efforts. It separates basic influencer marketing campaigns from true Winfluence. Without goals and a plan to measure them, you'll never know how you did, or be able to answer that big question of ROI.

🐾 DEFINE YOUR AUDIENCE

By now you know what you want to accomplish with your influence marketing program. The next step is to specifically define which audience or audience segment you'll focus on to achieve that goal. Here's where many business owners make a seemingly small mistake that affects their entire marketing program in a huge way.

Many business owners, and even some marketers, define their audience as "everyone." Every person can buy my product, so my target is everyone. But that is simply irrational thinking.

Simply put, *everyone* is not going to buy your product or service. In fact, not even everyone in your target demographic is going to buy it. But more of them will if you target your campaign well, perhaps even very specifically, and know exactly who your ideal customer is.

Why Get Specific?

There are three key reasons you should get specific when defining the audience for your influence marketing program. Each one leads to more effective use of your time and money and ultimately makes your effort more successful.

1. *The better defined your target audience is, the better decisions you'll make. Period.* Define your customers to understand who buys from you, where and when they buy, what they look and act like, what else they buy and from whom, where they spend time online, and what content they share there. The more you know about them—how they think, what they like—the easier it will be for you to put yourself in their place and persuade them to think or act as you want them to.

2. *Understanding your audience on a granular level helps you choose the types of influence partners you need to leverage for successful programs.* Influential people can be bloggers or Instagram users with a huge following, but they can also be influential current customers, journalists, industry thought leaders, or experts. In some cases, they might be celebrities. Each type is slightly different, but knowing

which kinds will work well for your campaign is a byproduct of understanding your target audience.

3. *Knowing your audience and the types of influence partners you need then helps you choose better partners.* As an example, clothing company Tom James has a very well-defined target consumer. The clothier's audience is broadly described as high-net-worth individuals, successful in business, driven, and image-conscious. They have a polished sense of style and accomplishment. They drive expensive cars, live in houses decorated by an interior designer, smoke Cuban cigars, and drink top-shelf whiskey. Their male clients wear pocket squares in their blazers that are coordinated with their tie and socks. Knowing this, the brand avoids partnering with influential people who post selfies in cargo pants and ball caps.

You cannot successfully pick the right types of individuals or even specific influence partners if you don't deeply understand the audience you're trying to reach. Consider your target audience one half of a Venn diagram. The influential person's audience is the other. You want as much overlap in that diagram as possible. But if you don't know who is in either side, you won't know if you've chosen the right audience, partner, or strategy.

DELINEATE INFLUENTIAL PEOPLE

You should now understand how knowing your audience helps the next step of delineating your influence partners. The Venn diagram example requires two pieces of information: your audience and the person with influence's audience. Once you know what their audience should look like, you can start identifying influential people you might want to work with.

In most cases, your intended audience is one that many people with influence will reach. If you sell eagle feather quill pens to bearded Russian librarians with halitosis, you probably already know the one guy who's influential online in that narrow niche. For the rest of you, as granular as your prescription might be, there will still be multiple people with influence to choose from.

Appendix A of this book includes a helpful guide and worksheet you can use to score and prioritize your influence partners. It gives you a numeric scale to score each individual influence partner using the reach, relevance, and resonance factors we'll discuss in Chapter 7.

What Are Good Choices for Influence Partners?

So what makes a good influence partner? The answer depends on a lot of different factors, including your program's goals. Some influence partners might be great at driving traffic but not very persuasive, so if your goal is to get people to visit your retail location, they probably aren't the best choice.

Remember what we talked about in Chapter 3: There's a difference between people who are influencers and those who have influence. Being able to distinguish between the two is key to this step of the process.

Ultimately, you have to ask who actually influences the people you wish to reach in the context of what you're asking for. If I'm handling the marketing for Topgolf and residents near the site of their proposed facility in Louisville, Kentucky, are up in arms over the disruption it would cause, enlisting those influential about golf won't help me. I need to engage community leaders, local issues bloggers, and even fellow residents.

Those who impact your audience in the right context may in fact be on the list of YouTube stars or popular Instagrammers spit out by your influence marketing software platform. But you can't rely on software alone. Its data is limited to online reach and engagement. Understanding how, or even if, that translates to real influence is a computation best left to your brain—which must consider off-line influences as well.

You also need to ensure the influential people you target are a good fit for your brand and can prove they are effective. We'll dive deeper into these issues in Chapter 7.

🔆 DEVELOP ASSETS

You know your audience. You've identified your ideal influence partners. But your job is just beginning. Before you contact individuals about your campaign, you should fully understand what you'll ask each to do to meet the goals of the project. In other words, you need to anticipate what resources, content, images, videos, and other assets they will need from you to pull it off.

Nothing kills a good influence campaign faster than getting the influence partner onboard and then saying, "Oh . . . um, well. It'll take us a week or so to gather up all the stuff you need. So hold on! We'll get back to you!"

The more prepared you are, the more successful your partners will be, and the more successful the engagement will be. That is why Chapter 8 is devoted to building your content arsenal.

DELIVER MESSAGES

Look back at what you've built to this point. That's a lot of work, isn't it? And yes, I know you're probably thinking, "Are we there yet, Dad?" At least in relation to the actual outreach. Well, we're there yet.

Now you're finally ready to reach out to your influence list, pitch them the big idea, get them onboard, and execute the program. But even the engagement piece requires planning in and of itself.

Some influential people are easy to reach. They publish their email address and sometimes even their phone numbers on their social channels or blogs. Others may wish to be approached publicly on their social channels or even called on the phone. Yes! Old school. Still others may not want to be bothered at all.

You need to prioritize and make notes on how you'll connect with each one.

Chapter 9 is all about this step—The Art of Engaging Those with Influence. Part III of the book dives deeper into the executional phase of influence marketing activation.

DETERMINE SUCCESSES

While measuring success is at the end of your list of things to do, you've heard me emphasize how important it is to plan ahead several times now. Sure, measurement, by definition, implies you're looking back on something that has already happened. However, to maintain a competitive edge in everything from pay-per-click (PPC) advertising to broadcast TV communications, measurement today is more focused on optimization, so you can improve your campaign while it's still in progress.

To be smarter about measurement, then—say it with me—you have to *plan to measure*. And you have to revisit your measurements early and often.

The good news is that Winfluence means planning to measure is already baked into the process. Think about the first of your "Six Ds." What did you start with? You decided your goals.

You can use all the analytics software you want, look at every chart and graph under the sun, and think about every number on every report you can find, but 99 percent of them will not produce evidence that you accomplished your goal.

Planning to measure, then, is as simple as identifying the analytics and reports that give you that evidence. And going back to look at them often to see how much closer you are to achieving that goal.

In Chapter 15, we'll take a more in-depth look at planning to measure so you can do this process well.

BUILD YOUR BLUEPRINT

The six steps to building influence marketing campaigns will help ensure you have a blueprint for success. With each campaign, you'll find that each step will be different from those before it. From building brand awareness to driving sales in a specific retailer and market, your influence marketing programs will need individual customization.

That's why each step has a corresponding chapter that expands on the ideas, illustrated with case studies and examples. It's important the steps are drilled into you throughout this book so they're easy for you to remember when you're finished reading.

Even with this high-level look at the blueprint for developing influence marketing campaigns, you're not quite ready to hit the ground running. But you will be once you figure out which influence partners to use and why.

To find out how to do that, I want to tell you my personal David and Goliath story.

IDENTIFYING THOSE WITH INFLUENCE

In 2008, there probably wasn't a bigger name in marketing technology than Robert Scoble. The blogger, who worked for Microsoft and was generally credited with being the human face of the corporate tech giant, had attracted ridiculous amounts of attention for his videos and blog posts reviewing tech companies and their software. *Fast Company* magazine finally gobbled him up to be the star of two shows on its new FastCompany.tv video network.

Every CEO in Silicon Valley wanted "Scobleizer" to talk about their software or other tech. One of those CEOs was Jonathan Spier of NetBase. His software was a social listening platform that would search blogs, news articles, social network posts, and more to find a company name or other keyword and organize those mentions into meaningful insights.

NetBase's customers could find out what people were saying about their company, their executives, their products, or even just topics they were interested in. Then NetBase would automatically score those mentions—let's call them conversations—for key topics and sentiments, pair those with known information about the source and author, and produce insights akin to the ones you could get from consumer focus groups or market research. If Robert Scoble talked about NetBase, Spier's company would immediately have the name recognition to demo its platform to a laundry list of big companies.

But when Kevin Cheng at Eastwick Communications, NetBase's PR firm at the time, ran a search for "social media software" through an influence marketing tool, Robert Scoble wasn't their only target. Because he covered broader topics than just social media software, he wasn't even the top name on the list. Someone else turned out to be a more influential person for NetBase's software.

It was me.

(I'm not trying to be self-aggrandizing here. But this story illustrates the point that choosing the right influence partner doesn't always mean going with the big-audience, sexy ones. Bear with me a moment. I promise this isn't an ego trip.)

The blog I was writing at the time, *Social Media Explorer*, was dialed in on social media technology. I was a PR pro who "got" social media. As a result, I was fascinated with social media monitoring and social listening software because I saw early on how it could inform your content marketing, surface consumer insights for R&D, and more.

I had already covered several other platforms emerging in the space on my blog, including a review of Radian6 and a discussion of Sysomos. My audience was a lot of PR and social media-focused communications professionals—the exact people who were interested in purchasing social listening software.

When analyzing its influence partners, NetBase looked at relevance, reach, and resonance—not just reach. The combination of those factors led them to decide I was the higher-priority target.

Cheng and NetBase CMO Lisa Joy Rosner reached out and asked me to do a demo. Spier would be on the call personally to show me the software. I was skeptical their platform could do what they claimed, but I agreed to see it in action. Midway through the call, Spier said, "Why don't we just show you a live instance of NetBase and search for something you're interested in?"

That was ballsy. He was offering to do a live demo right in front of someone who could potentially trash his new toy before it ever got started. Ask Elon Musk how that feels after his November 2019 launch of the Tesla Cybertruck. Musk bragged about the truck's bulletproof exterior and then watched lead designer Franz von Holzhausen throw not one but two metal balls at the truck, shattering both driver's side windows.

"OK," I said. "Search for Kentucky Fried Chicken." KFC, the Louisville-based gem of the Yum! Brands conglomerate, was in the news that week for pinkwashing—promoting chicken sales to raise money for breast cancer awareness through a special pink bucket. My friend Geoff Livingston had written a blog post berating the restaurant chain. While KFC wasn't a client, I defended them to Geoff and others, accusing them in turn of complaining about a company trying to do some good.

Spier typed in "Kentucky Fried Chicken," and a word cloud emerged, with big words representing higher volumes of conversation and smaller ones representing lesser concentrations of chatter. The phrases "KFC," "Colonel Sanders," and "chicken" were massive. The next biggest conversation rested in the lower middle of the cloud: "Pinkwashing." Just off to the side of that word was "Geoff Livingston." On the other side: "Jason Falls."

I almost fell out of my chair.

I posted my glowing review of NetBase the following week. Scoble published something about the company as well, as did several other bloggers who wrote about tech and social tools. "But it was your writeup that led to a comment which turned into a lead, and then a customer," Cheng told me recently.

NetBase's influence marketing software found a little-known influence prospect who turned out to be valuable to them. I wasn't Microsoft's original blogger, didn't host a couple of web TV shows for *Fast Company*, and didn't have hundreds of thousands of followers. I was a social media guy at an ad agency in Louisville. But I was one of the right influence partner targets for NetBase. Within a month of my blog post, NetBase signed a major brand to a seven-figure contract.

But before we get too deep into thinking there are "right" people of influence and "wrong" people of influence, let's clarify. Yes, there will be some people you don't want to partner with. Everything from the geography of their audience to the topics they focus on and how professional (or unprofessional) their content is can make them a "wrong" choice for you.

However, for the sake of this discussion, I'm assuming that you're always going to start with a list of influence targets that are potentially "right." Whether you begin by filtering them by geography, industry, topic, or network, let's assume you don't have any "wrong" influence targets but only "right" and "more right" ones. Even the ones who don't align perfectly with you can scream from the rooftops that they love your business, which probably can't hurt.

The challenge, then, is to develop a list of "more right" influence partners and prioritize them beginning with the "most right" on down. This chapter will outline how to do this.

HOW DO YOU FIND GOOD INFLUENCE PARTNERS?

Finding the right influence partners depends on a lot of different factors, including the goals of your program. Some partners might be great at driving traffic, but not very persuasive, so if you want to get people to visit your retail location, they're probably not the best choice.

Remember what we talked about in Chapter 3: There's a difference between people who are influencers and people who have influence. Being able to delineate that is key to this step of the process.

Now let's take this one step further and make it absolutely clear: There is a BIG difference between influence and popularity.

Take hamburgers, for instance. There are people who know a lot about hamburgers. They know how to choose the right meat, season it appropriately, cook it on different surfaces, choose the best condiments and side dishes, and more.

You could say that Guy Fieri is influential when it comes to hamburgers. He's a celebrity chef, owns several restaurants that sell them, and has offered outstanding recipes for them on his TV shows. Someone who is building a Winfluence strategy to sell hamburgers would pick someone like him as a relevant person of influence.

However, in March 2018, Burger King announced the face of its new marketing efforts would be UFC's Conor McGregor. Is McGregor influential? Certainly. As of this writing, the Irish fighter has more than 32 million followers on Instagram alone.

But what does he know about hamburgers? He might know how to make someone's face *look* like hamburger, but he doesn't bring credibility to the table when it comes to cooking them. McGregor's popularity online is irrelevant to his influence (or lack of it) in the fast-food space.

For your influence marketing programs to be Winfluence programs, they have to successfully deliver business value beyond mere impressions or reach. For that, you need to add a layer of context and relevance to your selection process. Popularity is simply a head count of how well-known a person is. But will their fans trust what they have to say or respond to a message that says, "Go do this" or "Go try this"?

Advertising research has continually shown that celebrity endorsements like McGregor's don't have much impact on consumers. That effect is even more pronounced in the influence marketing space.

Collective Bias is one of the original influence marketing agencies, which became known in the mid-2000s for developing programs like the Walmart Moms, a group of bloggers who acted as brand ambassadors for the retail giant. The firm surveyed 1,500 adults in 2018 and found that 34 percent would consider buying a product endorsed by their peers, but only 3 percent would do so based on a celebrity's endorsement. In other words, more than ten times as many individuals would rely on the word of people they knew over a celebrity.

The celebrity also needs credibility around the topic to have influence over their audience. Think about Arii, the Instagram influencer in Chapter 3 who couldn't sell a few dozen T-shirts to her followers. She's popular, but would you pay her to try to move a few hundred SKUs of your product? Probably not.

By this point, you should have confirmed the influence partners you're considering reach your target audience or segment. But you also need to ask whether their content will actually appeal to that audience. Reach is important, but so is relevance.

GOOD INFLUENCE PARTNERS MAKE BRAND SENSE

Does a potential influence partner's content align with your brand in a relevant way? Dorrie Jacobson posts on Instagram as @seniorstylebible. Her audience on that platform numbers more than 40,000; on Facebook it's about 30,000; and on Pinterest she has about 8,000 monthly viewers. Jacobson, who is in her mid-80s, shows off the height of fashion for senior women on her account. Her content is consistent—and consistently good. Her audience is engaged and responsive to her calls to action.

But asking Jacobson to help communicate the benefits of cholesterol medicine or assisted living facilities, even though those topics are highly relevant to the demographic she serves, simply wouldn't resonate well with her audience. It's not the type of content they are used to seeing from her. Unless she introduced the topics with personal stories of how they impacted her life, her audience would not be likely to engage.

But if GE Appliances asked Jacobson to help spread the word about its Great American Grandma job search—which it did in February 2019—the chances of success are better. It's not fashion-specific content, but the call for applicants for its position promoting social media asked for "stylish" and "hip" grandmothers from all walks of life. Jacobson's audience fit the profile of who GE Appliances was looking for, and her content helped drive more than 200,000 impressions of the job search. GE ultimately received 700 applications for the job.

GOOD INFLUENCE PARTNERS DELIVER AND PROVE IT

Another good way to judge popularity vs. influence is to look at previous sponsored content the person with influence has posted. Quickly searching through their feed for any posts that contain #ad, #client, #sponsored, or similar tags should bring up relevant posts. Do they look appealing, present compelling calls to action, and appear effective? If so, it's likely this person might be a good fit.

I've seen fantastic, engaging organic content from influential people, only to see sponsored posts fall flat. They're good to *their* audience, but they underserve *yours*.

One example I came across in 2019 was an influential person driving deep, emotional content around health and wellness. It was the kind of inspirational content people see in their feed and get excited about. Then, right in the middle of her feed, was a picture of her holding a bottle of water with copy that basically said, "I love the taste of this water. You should try it."

That won't motivate anyone to try the water. It's like she's giving her audience a wink-wink, nudge-nudge to say, "Gotta spam you with this to pay the mortgage. You know how it is. Just ignore this and move along."

Choose influence partners who make it possible for brands *and their audience* to make a connection and who motivate their followers to trust the brand, because they trust the person.

Good influence partners will also prove they provide value by giving you metrics to show they can accomplish what you want. They run their Instagram accounts, blogs, YouTube channels, and Pinterest boards like a business. They understand the power of their audiences and the business behind connecting brands to that audience. And they understand you can't work with them if they cannot demonstrate the value they provide.

GOOD INFLUENCE PARTNERS MEET YOUR GOALS

We discussed three reasons to get specific when defining your audience in the previous chapter. You need to apply the same fine-toothed comb when analyzing the influential people you're considering as partners.

You have identified the people with true influence, rather than just popularity. You've chosen the ones who are contextually relevant to your brand and who will deliver the business metrics you need to justify your investment.

But which ones in that group are the right ones in content and style to deliver the goals you want to accomplish? Assume none of them are like the passive "Drink this water" endorser I mentioned above. Your list is full of smart, strong, interesting, and potentially effective influence partners.

Which of them can push the right buttons to drive more sales or traffic, better engagement, or changes in opinions? Which ones are Winfluencers?

If your primary goal is page views or website traffic, focus on the size of the influential person's audience so you get maximum reach. If you want to drive more sales or email subscribers, choose influence partners who are more persuasive and can talk their audience into doing specific things. And if your goal is something like building backlinks for SEO purposes, pick partners with high-authority websites.

The more specific you can get when matching your audience to your influence partners, the better your influence marketing effort will fare.

THE WINFLUENCE PRIORITY SCORECARD

Take a look at Figure 7-1 on page 95, which is a working example of the Winfluence Priority Scorecard. I have included a blank one for you to use in Appendix A at the end of this book. This helpful worksheet allows you to score each possible influence partner and then compare all the ones on your list to see who should be prioritized for outreach.

The scorecard is based on the same pillars of analysis NetBase used in its software: reach, relevance, and resonance. It should be used by first filtering your analysis by your overall program goal, and then by the scale of your program. Your analysis of an influence prospect for a global awareness campaign will have a different score from the same person analyzed for a local sales effort, so you have to filter it through those perspectives from the start.

You can see the example is for the influence prospect The Bar-B-Queue, a fictional local restaurant reviewer who posts on Twitter,

figure 7–1. An Example of a Winfluence Priority Scorecard

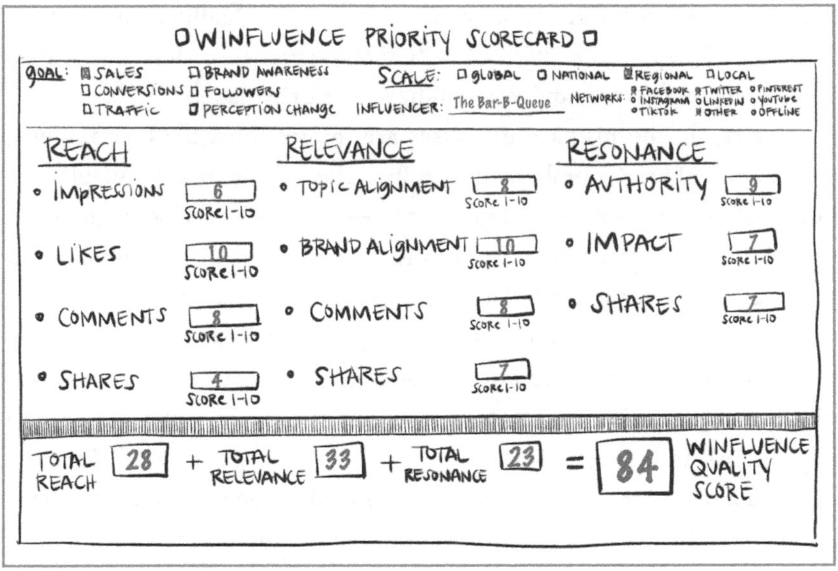

Facebook, and a blog, which is why "Other" is checked. The goal of my program is sales, so I'm hoping to partner with people with influence who will drive people to my new burger joint. This particular influence prospect's content aligns well with my brand voice and audience, so they score a 10 for brand alignment. They don't have a huge audience, so they have a lower impressions score (6) than others on my list, but they have a higher percentage of likes and comments than others, so they score well there, too (10 and 8, respectively).

The scorecard lists the primary factors you can measure with online influencers, or score yourself, within each of the columns. These are meant to be rated on a 1 to 10 scale, based on your analysis of that influence prospect or in comparison to the others on your list. So if you have ten influence prospects and you know how many comments each one drives on an average post, the one with the most comments would receive a score of 10 for the comments category, the second-highest would receive a 9, and so on.

When you're done, add up each column to get an overall score for reach, a score for relevance, and a score for resonance. Add up those three, and you have that influence prospect's Winfluence Quality Score (WQS). The Bar-B-Queue has a WQS of 84. Compare each influence partner on your list by their WQS, and you will have a priority list.

For reach, the primary measures are impressions, likes, comments, and shares. These numbers generally reflect how many people are impacted by the person's content. For relevance, or how closely aligned a given influence partner is to your brand, I've listed topic alignment, brand alignment, comments, and shares. Resonance is a judgment of whether the influence partner's content is meaningful to the audience you're trying to reach. The factors there are authority (in the industry or topic your program aligns with), impact (how well they can motivate the audience to take action), and shares.

You'll notice content shares are listed in all three categories. I believe that is the ultimate social media content metric, the online equivalent of word of mouth. If someone likes the content enough, they'll proactively share it with their networks, especially if they add commentary to the share to explain why they're sharing it. That means the content reached them, was relevant to them, and resonated with them.

You can learn more about the Winfluence Priority Scorecard and WQS at winfluencerbook.com.

INFLUENCE MARKETING SOFTWARE

By now you know I believe off-line influence matters as much as online. But when you need to find those good influence partners on social networks like YouTube, Instagram, TikTok, and others, software is your friend.

Eastwick used a program called Traackr to identify and prioritize NetBase's list of potential influence partners. Relatively new to the space in 2008, Traackr is now one of the standard-bearers for software as a service (SaaS) products identifying influential people online.

But there are hundreds of other software platforms designed to identify, prioritize, and, in some cases, even communicate with and manage online influence prospects. The general approach is simple: Enter a number of criteria for the influence targets you are looking for, and a list of potential matches appears. You can then review, add, or remove individuals, search again with different filters, and so on, until you are happy with your list of prospective influence partners.

Then, depending on the complexity of the software, you may be able to save your list, perform outreach to the people on the list one by one or en masse, track communications, provide assets, and even measure social metrics for their posts.

As you can imagine, having software do all this is amazing and can save you hours and hours of time. But it comes at a cost.

The more advanced influence marketing platforms (Traackr, Mavrck, Onalytica, Julius/HYPR) cost in the low thousands of dollars per month to use. Some agency or marketplace platforms like IZEA or Tribe operate as a blend of software and professional services, where the company can do all the work for you based on your goals and project briefs. They're generally more expensive, though some, like IZEA, also have software-only offerings that are competitively priced.

There are also midlevel SaaS solutions, like Mention, BuzzSumo, TapInfluence, and Klear, that typically cost between $25 and $500 per month. These offer only software, not professional services, and some are very limited on what they actually analyze to determine influence. Some are simple scrapes of Twitter data, surfacing the people with the most followers who have your given keyword in their bio. That won't help you with influential people on Instagram or YouTube. When it comes to influence marketing software, you generally get what you pay for.

As of this writing, Cornett has one client that uses IZEA for large-scale influence programs. We have another that leverages a service-software hybrid platform called Fohr. Within our agency, our core influence marketing suite of software includes IZEA, Julius/HYPR, and BuzzSumo.

We do most of our research and list building in Julius/HYPR. For outreach and campaign management, we focus on individual relationship building, with an emphasis on old-fashioned email and one-on-one communications.

For up-to-date information about influence marketing tools, including customer ratings and reviews, I highly recommend the site G2, which collects curated ratings and reviews of all kinds of technology and allows you to compare and contrast your options. Find the influence marketing tools at www.g2.com/categories/influencer-marketing.

SOFTWARE ALONE IS NOT THE SOLUTION

I'm sure the various sales teams at these software companies would love for me to finish this chapter by saying the way to find the "more right" influence partners is to use software. But finding the right influential people for your business, brand, product, or event can never be left to software alone (not to mention that some budgets won't support software at all).

Why can't you just rely on software? Because that's the easy way out. That's not Winfluence. You're not looking for a broad list of influence targets that *might* be right. You're looking for a curated list of influential people that are *more right*. I've yet to see an algorithm that can split the hairs of nuance between one person and another when all the main filters are set correctly. I'll dive deeper into my philosophy and reasoning in Chapter 16.

So how do you zero in on the "more right" influence partners? The first rule of marketing is to know your audience. Remember our discussion in Chapter 6 about defining your audience? The better defined your target audience is, the better decisions you'll make when building your influence marketing campaigns.

Yes, a lot of what we're talking about in this book is focused on online influencers. But remember our overall point: This isn't about influence marketing, but Winfluence. You have to continually revisit the idea that the people with real influence over your prospective customers might be people who are close to them in the real world: community leaders, behind-the-scenes trendsetters, ministers, members of the traditional media, academics, conference keynote speakers, workshop leaders, or even the successful local Arbonne independent consultant.

You know who perhaps the most connected people in a given community typically are? Life insurance reps. I mean, have you ever been to a networking event in your town where you didn't meet a Northwestern Mutual "associate"?

Joking aside, whether it's your given industry, your local community, or a network of schools or nonprofits, the people with the most influence over the audience you're trying to reach may not have Instagram accounts, YouTube channels, or even much online presence at all. Keep that in mind every step of the way.

And don't worry. I'll remind you of this many more times before the end of the book.

You can still use the Winfluence Priority Scorecard in Appendix A for off-line influence partners. You'll just need to be creative with how you apply ratings to the scorecard factors to make sure their off-line reach score is comparable to someone with similar impact online.

You can better understand how to rate people with off-line influence in comparison to those online by digging deeper into understanding your audience. You can do this by analyzing their 'tudes.

THE FIVE KEY 'TUDES OF YOUR AUDIENCE

The right people with influence begin to emerge when you study the five key 'tudes of your audience, as shown in Figure 7–2 below.

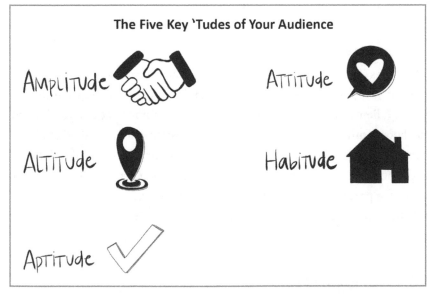

figure 7–2. The Five Key 'Tudes of Your Audience

Dude, what are the 'tudes? I'm glad you asked!

🤝 Amplitude of Audience

Based on your business goals, does your audience need to be big? If you want 50 million people to see your name by Monday, take out a Super Bowl ad and hope the big game is this Sunday. But if you want to persuade legislators to support your stance on the state's casino gambling laws, you don't necessarily need to engage an influence partner with 2 million followers. You need an influential person followed by a few dozen state representatives and senators.

📍 Altitude of Audience

Think about this in terms of geography. If you need to influence employees inside your company, that Instagrammer with 250,000 followers probably isn't your best choice, even if they post content your employees dig. John Chamberlin and Rachael Rennebeck of YaJagoff! (yajagoff.com), a blog, podcast, and website focused on Pittsburgh, are great influence prospects with 50,000-plus followers, but they're not useful if you own a single-location business in Birmingham, Alabama.

✓ Aptitude of Audience

This is less about the audience's intelligence and more about the complexity of what you're trying to persuade them to do or know. If you want to help your audience understand the process of water purification, you'll need to choose influence partners who can build instructional and educational content. If you're trying to persuade people to buy a high-quality kitchen appliance that is 50 percent more expensive than its competition, your influence partners will need to be able to get into the weeds of why yours is better. Someone who just posts pictures of beautiful kitchen designs may not help you.

❤ Attitude of Audience

Do the people you hope to ultimately influence love you? Do they hate you? Do they not even really know you? Their attitude toward you can drastically change which influence partners are right for you. If they hate you, some rah-rah cheerleader type who just smiles and waves off any negative vibes won't work. You need partners with deep levels of trust from their audience who are willing to work on changing attitudes with you.

 Habitude of Audience

What is the audience's usual way of doing things? And, to use a play on words, what channels do they inhabit? If you're trying to reach IT professionals who manage data servers, your influence partners will likely need to be present and impactful on blogs, YouTube, IT forums, and message boards. If you're trying to reach consumers of just about anything in Japan, Twitter and Line are far more important for your influence partners than, say, Facebook. Japanese consumers are culturally less likely to engage when their real identity is tied to the account, while Facebook norms are for each person to have one account under their real name. Twitter allows you to have a handle and represent yourself however you like.

THE FINAL FILTER FOR PRIORITIZING YOUR PEOPLE OF INFLUENCE

Once you've studied the 'tudes and identified individuals that meet those qualifications, it's time to start asking questions about them. Here are the five I tend to focus on:

1. *Do they truly reach my target audience or segment?* The influence partner with the largest following in most cities may check all the 'tude boxes: right-size network, right place of influence, perfect to communicate the complexity of our message, no concern about the audience's attitude, and their impact is mostly on YouTube. But if I'm an office supply store in Grand Rapids, Michigan, Franceska Boerman's 85,000 YouTube subscribers, who show up to watch her wedding and fitness videos, won't do me a lot of good. Latasha James, however, has 22,000 YouTube subscribers who enjoy her business coaching and marketing videos. Both are big in Grand Rapids, but James is "more right" for my business.

2. *Does their content appeal to my target audience or segment?* Again, the 'tudes check out. My list of influencer partners does reach the intended audience. But does that audience find their content appealing? This isn't a dumb question. Just because someone follows an influence prospect or their content reaches the person doesn't preclude the person from skipping over the person's content. Do members of your prescribed audience actually engage with their content? Are you finding comments, shares, or recommendations that stem from the content? Remember, reach is one thing— resonance is another.

3. *Does their content align with my brand?* What do you think of when you hear the brand name BMW? Most people think luxury, premium, expensive, classy. So would Iggy Pop make a good brand spokesperson? Probably not. He even proved as much during an appearance at the Cannes Lions Festival in 2016, saying, "If BMW hired me, if I was writing the copy, I'd go, 'THIS IS A FUCKING BMW! SHUT UP AND BUY THE FUCKING CAR, WHAT THE FUCK, ALL RIGHT?! BUY IT!'" That doesn't sound like BMW at all. When you look at the influence prospect's content, would it fit in an ad for your company? Do they look and feel like your company or its customers? If not, consider moving them off or down the priority list.

4. *Does their other sponsored content appear compelling, engaging, and relevant?* Brass tacks here, folks: You want to engage with influence partners who can move the needle. See if they have done the same for other brands they've worked with. No, you don't have access to other people's financial statements or success metrics. But you can see those sponsored posts or brand mentions and judge if the content is appealing, interesting, and generally aligned with the company. You can see the comments, shares, and some vanity metrics. You can also see if there are multiple posts with the same brand—a good sign the brand was happy with the first ones.

5. *Can they illustrate they provide value?* This is tricky to know before reaching out to the influence partner, but many savvy ones post

media kits and sponsorship information on their websites or blogs. The really savvy ones share some level of measurement to indicate how effective they are beyond reaching eyeballs. While few will share the full gamut openly, some will offer metrics like average clickthrough rate, average engagement rate, or quotes from previous clients about the program's success.

As a follow-up to the question of whether an influence prospect provides value, I recommend spending some time with each one's content. You can follow them and look for new posts over the course of a few days or weeks, but also scroll back on their feeds and decide whether they are someone you should align yourself with.

Look at their pronouns. Do they say "I," "me," and "mine" more than "you" or "yours"? Influential types who name-drop and brag tend to lose their audience's interest over time. Those who create value for their audience tend to be more trustworthy and persuasive.

While we'll dive deeper into your relationship with influence partners in Chapter 9, there are also some qualities you need to be mindful of when you reach out and contact the influence prospects to decide whether they're "more right" for you.

Do they try to understand your business and your goals for the engagement? Remember that we've reached a point in the evolution of influence marketing where brands no longer just throw money at YouTubers and Instagrammers and live with whatever they get in return. You are practicing Winfluence. You are investing in a marketing execution and must be able to measure the success of that investment.

The "more right" influence partners want to understand what success looks like for you so they can better produce it. They will also share success metrics from their social and website channels transparently and without hesitation. Smart influence partners know that happy brands come back for more campaigns, so they work to make you happy.

As you pitch to your priority list of influence partners, focus on asking questions that will help you understand whether they values their audience, as well as their relationship with you.

THE PAYOFF OF USING YOUR CIRCLES OF INFLUENCE

Don't forget there are many different types of people with influence. You probably come into contact with many influential people every day. You just don't think of them as "influencers."

Remember the circles of influence we discussed in Chapter 4? Figure 4-1 on page 44 showed us varying levels of people around your brand you can consider as potential audiences for influence. Your brand is at the center. The closest circle of influence is your employees, then vendors and partners, then current customers, and so on. All these people can then influence others about your brand in turn. Some of them are influential online, but many others influence their audiences off-line. It is wise, then, to put yourself through the exercise of identifying people of influence besides the stereotypical social media personalities with online followings.

A project Cornett ran for the University of Kentucky HealthCare team in 2019 focused on driving views, comments, and shares around a brand video. The team engaged several relevant local online influence partners to like, comment on, and share the spot. They did the same with off-line people of influence, like Lexington Mayor Linda Gorton and other elected officials, leaders of local civic organizations, a popular local dentist, and the music director at a large church in the city.

But they had started their influence program even before they hired us. UK HealthCare first screened the "We Are Proof" video to internal audiences and rallied their employees around the launch. The team also reached out to previous patients and their families who had positive stories to share about UK HealthCare.

They asked each group to visit the brand's Facebook page on the day the video launched, view it, and then like, comment, and share it. When they shared the video, they were asked to tell their UK HealthCare success story. By tapping into multiple circles of influence for the brand, a two-minute commercial for a hospital drove 40,000 views within the first few hours of being posted. After four days, it had hit 250,000 views. By the six-month mark, the video had been viewed more than 835,000 times.

The city of Lexington, where the hospital system is centered, only has a population of 323,000 people.

That campaign earned UK HealthCare and Cornett a 2019 Shorty Award (an award "honoring the best of social media") for Best in Pharma & Healthcare. It did so well because it leveraged Winfluence. Rather than simply choosing people with big online followings to amplify its campaign, UK HealthCare capitalized on its existing circles of influence to enlist employees, vendors, customers, and community members. Each became a channel of influence for the project regardless of how many online followers they had.

DON'T LOSE SIGHT OF RIGHT

If you haven't figured it out yet, quality over quantity is a prevailing theme in this book. For $1 million, you can have Kim Kardashian post a single image with a caption on Instagram. But if your goal is to earn sales or conversions for your business, her audience will have to manually type in your URL, unless Kim gives you the single link in her Instagram bio for the day or agrees to a shoppable post. Without that third-party add-on feature typically paid for by the brand engaging the influence partner, Instagram doesn't allow for hyperlinks.

The most generous conversion rate from this investment would be, let's say, 0.01 percent. And that's a huge stretch! There are just too many steps between the message and the conversion. That's 1,520 conversions from Kardashian's 152 million fans from a $1 million investment. Your average sale would have to be $658 to break even, and it would need to be more than $1,600 to account for overhead, if you follow the standard 2.5-times-cost formula.

For $5,000, you can probably find five to ten influence targets with modest audiences of 10,000 to 50,000 followers who will post your brand's call to action multiple times. They'll appreciate the engagement so much that you might even get free posts from time to time as you build the relationship. No, you may not get 1,520 people to rush out and buy your product, but if you got close, even if your product cost $10 you'd still make enough to account for overhead.

In Chapter 3, we talked about Robert Cialdini's explanation of the pressure consumers are under to surrogate authority—how the "rush of modern life" forces people to associate authority and credibility with superficial or even irrational cues. Remember that people are clamoring to follow online influencers because they don't have the time or energy to stop and carefully analyze who is giving them advice, information, or perspective. They're too busy.

In that chapter, we learned the first of two ways Cialdini's theory can help your influence marketing: by understanding why consumers appreciate those people with influence in their lives. Their behavior validates your investment of time and energy into influence marketing.

The second way to leverage the same idea is to not fall into a trap of efficiency when you are selecting your influence targets. It's easy to look at the Instagram profile or Facebook page of someone with 250,000 or more followers and think, "Wow! That's one heck of an influence partner. Put them on the list!"

It's *not* easy to remember that 250,000 fans mean nothing if the influence partner can't motivate them to do what you need them to do for your brand. You have to go beyond the surface and dig deeper into their authority credentials.

Consumers want to skip the deep research to save time. If *you* skip the deep research, you'll likely lose money. And we're not talking about losing here. We're talking about Winfluence.

BUILDING A
CONTENT ARSENAL

September 14, 2001, could have been just another day of pundits, radio hosts, and late night talk show comedians poking fun at the often awkward, deer-in-headlights moments of President George W. Bush. But that day came three days after the worst terrorist attack on U.S. soil, and the president had arrived at Ground Zero—the site of the destroyed towers of the World Trade Center—to see the destruction that had left so many hearts similarly shattered.

President Bush did not go there planning to make a speech. He went to shake hands and show symbolic support of the firefighters, police officers, emergency responders, and volunteers working diligently to find survivors, recover the bodies of those lost in the attack, and begin to pick up the pieces of a broken America.

His advisors had decided the night before that public remarks would not be a good idea. Bush wasn't known to be the best orator, and this was perhaps the most sensitive moment in modern U.S. history.

But once on site, the workers wanted to hear from their commander-in-chief. Bush climbed up on a crumpled fire engine half-buried in the rubble, put his arm around a fireman, lifted a bullhorn, and began to address the crowd as best he could.

"Louder!" someone yelled. Bush repeated his last line. As he began to move the bullhorn so those to the side and behind him could also hear, someone farther away yelled, "We can't hear you!"

Bush then uttered a few sentences that turned the world, and his place in it, upside down. He said: "I can hear you! I can hear you! The rest of the world hears you! And the people who knocked these buildings down will hear all of us soon."

The Bullhorn Speech is perhaps the most famous example of impromptu rhetoric in politics. Yes, the second half of Martin Luther King Jr.'s "I Have a Dream" speech was extemporaneous, but he'd given a version of the speech months earlier and knew the content, while performing its perfect oration off the cuff.

Regardless, none of us are likely to produce such high-quality content without significant preparation or resources. Neither will the people of influence we hope to use. We have to give them something to work with.

In this chapter, I will outline the importance of providing content to your chosen influence partners so they can give you the results you're seeking. You will learn the different types of content influence partners want or need to be successful. You will also better understand how to leverage content to get more out of them.

BUILD YOUR ARSENAL

Your job at this point is to build a content arsenal. Yes, you are likely engaging your influence partner to create content for or about you. But the good ones don't whip up magic influential posts out of thin air. They rely on you for tools they can use to communicate the message, even if it's just background information. They survey what's available and create the content you've asked for. The more tools at their disposal, the more creative, and successful, they can be.

Think of it like public or media relations of the past. You reach out to reporters with a story idea. You give them a press release; maybe supply them with logos, pictures, video assets, and quotes from various people; and hope they write or talk about your thing. Influence marketing isn't all that different.

Prepare the Toolbox

You now need to answer a lot of questions about your influence marketing program:

* Will the campaign be completely online, or will it also have an offline element?
* What types of background material do you have, or do you need to create, to ensure your influence partners are fully briefed on the goal, the messaging, and other details of the program?
* What assets do you have, or do you need to create, that can help communicate the message visually through images, graphics, or videos, or even through audio formats, slide decks, or multimedia elements?
* What assets will you use to populate content on your channels about the topic, vs. what you'll want your influence partners to employ?
* Do you want to post content that influential people then direct their audiences to, rather than having them post the content as original elements on their own channels?

You've seen me use the word "granular" a lot in this book. The more detailed you can be with these plans, the better your chance of success. Think of all sorts of content elements for your arsenal, like:

* Blog posts/articles
* White papers/books
* Webinars/seminars
* Presentations/slide decks
* Images/graphics
* GIFs/cinemagraphs
* Videos/interviews
* Instagram/Facebook Stories
* Infographics/data visualizations
* Consumer research/user data

You are essentially listing anything other than the opinion or perspective of the influence partners you've chosen to be part of your program. Spoon-feed your partners everything you can, but let them decide which parts to use. Why? Because the easier you make it for the influence partner to participate, the more enthusiasm they will have for your project and the higher the likelihood they'll deliver the results you're hoping for.

You'll also need to think about the tools and channels you can use to make or distribute the content. Consider whether you want to use:

* Your blog or website
* Digital asset manager or file sharing platform
* Video hosting or sharing services
* Audio hosting or sharing services
* Intranets or internal communications platforms
* Mail or shipping services

Planning not just your content arsenal but also the logistics of delivering that content to your influence partners before any outreach occurs will ensure a smoother, more professional operation.

Your content arsenal planning should go well beyond just whether, or how, you will provide your partners with access to your product or service. It also has to provide the necessary resources to ensure they know exactly what you want them to say, what benefits you wish them to focus on, and what call to action you'd like them to use.

Anticipate Your Influence Partners' Needs

Let's say I'm a B2B company leveraging influence marketing to change perceptions of my brand. The marketplace sees me as just a supplier of commodity equipment to the industry, but my company is actually highly skilled in offering technology solutions—software to complement the hardware. I need help getting that word out.

For the sake of argument, let's say I've been making and selling wire shelving units for big warehouses for the past 20 years. But over the past five years, my company has expanded to provide software solutions to index and catalog the supplies or products stored on those shelves, including robotic equipment to shelve and retrieve items from anywhere in the warehouse.

My main buyers—procurement professionals, facilities managers, logistics managers—turn a deaf ear when my sales team starts talking software or logistics because they know us as the shelf company. That's all we are, as far as they're concerned.

My challenge is to convince them we are more than that. Instead of talking about shelves, I have to talk to them about their problems in the warehouse—safety, efficiency, organization—but they need to hear it from someone besides my sales team.

First, I identify 20 to 30 people my buyers pay attention to and engage them to help re-educate their audiences about the solutions my brand provides. Some of them have videocentric content (YouTube, IGTV, or Stories), so they will need video content from me. Others are bloggers and podcasters who use Twitter a bit, so they need access to information, interviews, and maybe images to use on their posts. And a couple of them frequently speak at conferences and industry webinars, so content in slide decks is important.

Imagine if I had already engaged these influential voices, with the campaign set to launch next week, but I hadn't yet built my content arsenal to provide them with the necessary assets? I'd die a fast death, smothered by content deadlines.

So what do I need to have on hand *before* I reach out? Remember that I need to frame my solutions within the context of their audience's problems:

* Background research and information on warehouse safety
* Research and estimates on productivity lost due to warehouse logistics and organization
* Videos of my company leadership or potential clients talking about these problems
* Images and quotes from those videos for use in print or on blogs that don't use video
* Case studies and examples of warehouses that have improved productivity and safety with automated systems

And that's the list of assets I'm pulling together just to help my influence partners frame the problem. Granted, if you pick incredibly relevant people of influence for your program, they may have already created some of the content you need. But assuming they have it ready will kill your credibility with them if they don't, so be prepared to supply it.

Now let's talk about the assets I need to connect the solution to these problems to my shelving company:

* Videos of any happy clients talking about their problems, followed by our solution
* Videos of my company leadership explaining how and why our solution works
* Images and quotes from those videos for use in print or on blogs that don't use video
* Images of the robotics equipment, enabled shelving, or warehouse space
* Videos of the robotics equipment seeking, finding, and retrieving stored items
* Product sheets and pricing information
* Talking points broken down into sound bite bullet points for easy learning and recall (in case my influence partners do podcast or video interviews about it)

* Instructions and related assets for calls to action I've planned to measure

Will my influence partners use every bit of that content? Probably not. But without it, they're less capable of telling the story I need them to tell and convincing their audience that my company is not just an old shelf vendor.

Anticipate Their Audience's Needs

In general, reactions to the influence partner's content associated with programs like these are positive and enthusiastic. But the content may prompt questions or comments from the influence partner's audience, and you need to prepare them to respond.

In our above example, it wouldn't surprise me if audience members commented on an influential person's post, asking, "Why is a shelving company trying to sell robots?" Or even pushing back on the notion of automating warehouse jobs, which might mean laying off hardworking employees.

It's one thing to develop content with the intent to inform, entertain, or persuade. It's an entirely different thing to develop communications strategies should that content not be well-received. This is where your public relations or corporate communications team members or partners can help. They're used to anticipating media pushback and steering those conversations in more positive, or at least neutral, directions.

You may be thinking this is an awful lot of planning and work just to engage some influential people to create content. But do you really want a popular Instagrammer or YouTuber, or even a third-party industry thought leader, handling objections to your product or service without your input? I didn't think so.

Be sure to think through what the influence partner's audience might have to say about the content. Prepare some responses or ideas to give the partner as additional ammunition to fight any detractors. The more you can help them carry on the conversation with reasons to believe in you and your product, the smarter they will look and the more they will appreciate your support.

ANTICIPATE BEING FLEXIBLE

Regardless of how well you plan, how much content you create, how well-versed the influence partners are in your brand, or how many resources you put at their disposal, something you didn't anticipate will always come up. It's just the nature of the beast. In traditional media relations, public relations, or influence marketing, you can't be everything to everyone all the time.

And, if your influence partners are viewed as thought leaders within their space, they'll routinely be asked to do interviews, podcasts, TV shows, and even conference speeches. When those arise, they may turn to you for additional content or resources.

In my experience as a person of influence in the marketing space, I lost count of how many software clients I had to take aside and say, "I'm doing a guest post on someone else's blog. Can you produce a graph based on some data from [their topic of interest] so I have an excuse to talk about your platform?"

Obviously, when they refuse or are unable to help me, they lose the opportunity to be mentioned as a resource, perhaps score a valuable inbound link, and extend the value they were getting out of their partnership with me.

If you haven't noticed by now, my preference for influence marketing is to build long-term relationships with your most valuable partners over time. Ideally, those partners will continually turn to you for more content and resources so they can help carry your brand message forward, if only to provide additional value for the relationship. So being flexible and willing to serve your partner's ongoing needs can add to your return on the investment.

IF CONTENT IS KING, YOU BECOME A KINGMAKER

Building a content arsenal is imperative to make your influence partners look good and make it easy for them to carry your message forward. But it brings two key additional benefits to your brand. The first involves giving a boost to your partners that pulls you along with it. The other is a direct benefit to your brand.

Anyone who knows anything about marketing—online or otherwise—will tell you that content is king. If you're the person supplying online (or off-line) influence partners with the content that makes them king of that particular topic or niche, that makes you the kingmaker.

A good influence partnership works both ways. The brand benefits because the influence partner tells the story the brand wants them to tell. The person of influence benefits because they can rely on the brand for information, resources, and content. These are things the public doesn't necessarily have access to, so it raises the credibility and trustworthiness of the influential person.

This scenario mirrors the PR-media relationships of past and present. Beat writers in a given industry usually know the PR representatives from the major companies and frequently tap into those relationships for answers to questions, resources, and even inside tips. Those with online influence are not that different and may enjoy having the inside track now and then.

The second hidden benefit to building that content arsenal is that you get to use it, too! Need a video to bring your blog post to life? You've already got one. Want to attack search engine rankings for an industry issue you can solve—like warehouse safety? You've got scads of research to form into a landing page for the search engines to chew on.

Your relationship with your influence partners should introduce you to their audiences as a trusted resource for the topics, products, and services you focus on. When those audiences click through to your website or reach out to your sales team, you already own a library of evidence to back up that reputation. Use it.

Now that you have a content arsenal, you're ready for the linchpin of the whole influence marketing process: reaching out and persuading the people on your list to become your influence partners.

THE ART OF ENGAGING THOSE WITH INFLUENCE

The Head & Shoulders advertising tagline "You never get a second chance to make a first impression" isn't an original line. History disagrees on who said it first. The debate is between playwright Oscar Wilde or singing cowboy Roy Rogers. It actually first appeared in a 1960s advertisement for Botany Bay suits. Regardless of where it originated, it has proved to be true in influence marketing.

If deep research to find the "more right" influence partners is where you save, or at least avoid losing, money, then deep research to nail your pitch to them is where you make money. Akin to success in public and media relations, influence marketing payoff often relies on the art of the pitch.

PR pros know all about the pitch. Media relations often centers on pitching story ideas to skeptical editors and overworked writers or producers. Pitching influence prospects isn't much different, but the dynamics of the pitch are. Traditional media members—writers, editors, and producers—follow those codes of ethics we discussed in Chapter 1. They were learned either in journalism school or by working in a world where there was a clear separation between editorial and advertising.

On the editorial side of the business, PR pros would try to get the media to write about their product, service, or initiative. If they succeeded, it was because the journalist agreed the idea was worth covering. No money changed hands. They earned the reward of being written about.

In advertising, someone from the company (not normally the PR pro) would buy an ad promoting the product, service, or initiative. The publication or broadcast was paid to communicate the company's message, as the company wished it to be communicated.

Until the world of social media, blogs, and online influencers came along, the editorial side of the aisle didn't take money to write about a company. That would be unethical.

But being paid to talk about a company's product, service, or initiative is how many online creators earn a living. If you approach them hoping for some free publicity, you'll be out of luck.

Still, pitching your ideas to your chosen influence prospects isn't as simple as messaging them with "Hey! We'd like to pay you for a post!" In fact, those messages are often ignored and deleted as spam. Remember, you're trying to build long-term relationships with these people You don't want your first impression to be "Ewww . . . they're gooey and drip with smarmy, transaction-based greed."

From the outset, the pay-to-play element sets influence marketing apart from public relations. While your long-term goal is to build relationships with influence partners that often result in plenty of earned placements over time, you have to understand a budget is necessary, as is having respect for their time and the value they provide through access to their audience.

In this chapter, I'll share my approach to pitching. I'll even show you actual emails I've used to persuade both media members and influence prospects to jump onboard and join the programs I've managed in the past. I'll also explain the best practices of reaching out to your targets, breaking the ice, and closing the deal.

THERE'S MORE RESEARCH TO DO

Before you make that first impression, you need to learn as much as you can about the influence prospect. The more research you can do before you pitch them, the better your first impression will be.

Let's assume that you've followed the advice in Chapter 7 and now you have a list of curated and prioritized influence partners for your program. You plan to reach out to every single one of them. But you want to be optimally prepared to pitch to them so your success rate will be high.

You'll want to know the following things about your influence prospects before you contact them:

* How often do they post sponsored content?
* What types of content (text, image, video) do they leverage for sponsored content?
* How do they engage their audience around the brands they've worked with before?
* What level of engagement do they receive on sponsored content vs. nonsponsored posts?
* Do they use sponsored content on multiple channels (Facebook, Instagram, YouTube, Twitter, TikTok, etc.)?
* Have they used contests or giveaways in their content at all? If so, how successful did they seem to be?

The answers to these questions will give you an idea of what works and what doesn't for that influence prospect. Pitching a video concept to someone who never uses video, for instance, will earn you a guaranteed "no thank you."

DON'T FORGET PEOPLE WITH REAL INFLUENCE

Here's another friendly reminder that we're talking about Winfluence, not just influence marketing. Remember to continually revisit the idea that the people with real influence over your prospective customers might be people who don't use that influence online. Remember, they might be elected officials, ministers, academics, nonprofit leaders, or industry conference speakers.

These influence partners are going to be a little more difficult to research and prepare for. You may need to do some good old-fashioned legwork to figure out how best to approach them.

Your research will likely require identifying people who know them, calling and asking questions, looking for mutual connections, and asking for an introduction. I've found that simply introducing yourself and being honest about why you're connecting with them often works.

Let's say I'm trying to stand out among my competitors in the supply chain software space. I know that P. Fraser Johnson, a professor at Western University in Canada, is an expert in the field who frequently speaks at conferences and events. But as far as I can tell, he has no social media presence at all. I might email or call him with this:

> *My supply chain software company has conducted some research around supply chain managers at more than 1,000 companies across verticals. Would you be interested in reviewing the research and perhaps using any insights you find valuable in your upcoming talks? We're not looking for an endorsement per se, but we would love to associate our name with you by providing you with useful data for your work and presentations.*

Of course, I might also try to locate some people who know the professor and find out more about him, his talks, and whether he has any corporate relationships before I reach out. No influence marketing software will help me find information about Johnson. I have to track him down off-line.

CREATING THE PITCH OPPORTUNITY

Before you deliver that all-important first impression and pitch to your influence target, you first have to create a connection to them. Ideally, you will have plenty of time to build a relationship before you pitch them. Getting to know your influence targets and allowing them to know you and respond positively to your interactions is far better than cold-calling (or emailing) them.

However, you may need to ramp up your influence program quickly and may not have time to lay a foundation of friendship first. Either way, you need their contact information.

Many online influencers provide their email addresses, phone numbers, and sometimes even instructions on how to pitch them on their blogs or social network pages. You can also follow or request connections with them on various social networks and then potentially use private or direct messages to reach them. If you are using influence marketing software or even a media database like Cision or Meltwater, a quick search could be all you need to find the appropriate contact information.

Keep in mind that some potential influence partners will openly welcome brand solicitation. Others aren't overt about it but are willing to talk. Some are completely uninterested in earning sponsorship dollars or making brand connections and don't understand why you're bothering them.

Still others don't want to be contacted by anyone at any time and loathe brands or businesses trying to "use" them to get to their audience. I recommend respecting their wishes and taking them off your list. Hell hath no fury like a self-righteous influencer scorned.

For those perhaps willing but hard-to-reach partners, it may take you some time to make a connection. You may have trouble finding their contact information, or when you do, you may find they aren't responsive to your pitch. Don't give up! You can still get their attention. You can:

* Follow them on social networks
* Read their blogs/watch their videos
* Like, share, and comment on their content
* Post a review/drop a LinkedIn Skill on their profile
* Engage them on their blog comments section or in conversations on their social network about their area of expertise

Doing these things over time—and sometimes it can just be a few days, not weeks—they will start to recognize your name or avatar. They may not understand why you're engaging with them. But if you keep doing it consistently and genuinely, the know-like-trust continuum emerges: They start to know you. Eventually they like you. Then they trust you.

By that point you'll probably have earned the right to say, "Hey! I'm doing a thing for my company (or client) that you might be interested in. Should I send you some more information? *I can if you're interested.*"

THE GIFT OF THE GOLDEN PHRASE

That last phrase is important. "If you're interested" are perhaps the most powerful three words in influence marketing. For that matter, they might be the most powerful three words in all of marketing. Why? Because they psychologically disarm the audience.

If you try to hard sell them on your program, they might be completely offended you've just turned to spamming them. The important "like" and even more important "trust" elements will disappear in a heartbeat.

But adding "if you're interested" allows them to think, "Oh, that must not be meant for me. I'm not interested."

It's a kind of magic.

I checked with my author friend Roger Dooley to see if there was a better explanation than magic. He's the man behind the blog Neuromarketing (www.neurosciencemarketing.com), which studies the way our brains respond to various methods of persuasion.

"It seems counterintuitive, but giving people a choice makes them more likely to be persuaded," he told me. "One particular phrase, 'But you are free [to choose],' has been tested so many times around the world that it even has its own acronym: BYAF. In one large compilation of studies that tested a request with and without the BYAF message, twice as many subjects complied when they were told they could choose. I think that 'if you're interested' could function in a similar way to BYAF."

Dooley added that "if you're interested" might also create cognitive dissonance for a "no" response because the implied message is that the influence target is not interested. He said in many experiments, planting the seed of an implied "no" increased conversion rates. Dooley said that if the reason for the rejection isn't for a lack of interest but something else, like a busy schedule, responses may improve.

Of course, tacking on "if you're interested" to your email, text, private message, or phone call isn't all you need to sell your pitch. But once the influence prospect expresses interest, you can follow up with more details and get down to business.

PRIORITIZING YOUR PARTNERS

While the pitch is a big first leg of the messaging trip, there are others to follow. Now you need to think about the paperwork. That includes everything from your budget to the actual copy you'll use in email outreach to partners.

Start by prioritizing your influence partners. There are the coveted ones at the top of your list, and there are existing relationships you are confident will help you along the way—and there are many in between. Some will have massive audiences. Others will reach just a few people you absolutely must connect with. Be sure to consider the reach and quality of each influence partner's audience vs. your goal.

Appendix A is the Winfluence Priority Scorecard. This gives you a worksheet you can use to score each influential person on your list based on the reach-relevance-resonance factors we discussed in Chapter 7. Use this worksheet to give each potential person of influence a Winfluence Quality Score (WQS) to help you prioritize your list.

You still have to account for one more factor in the prioritization, though. The most significant factor, and one that will be fluid as you reach out and confirm influence partner's participation, is how much you'll need to pay each of them.

DEFINING A BUDGET

Influential people, especially those online, rarely work for free today. Many have gotten savvy to how their social media account analytics compare to traditional advertising metrics like impressions, reach, and frequency. And their online content is often all or a significant part of their livelihood.

Influence fees vary greatly. Some have large online followings and charge hefty fees to put your message in front of them. It's said a single

Instagram post from Kim Kardashian will run you a cool $1 million. Others may partner for product samples or even insider access to brand representatives or information alone.

Ideally, you will use a mix of people with larger followings for awareness impact and smaller, more expert-level influence for impacts surrounding conversions. However, be prepared to pay for being presented to their audiences.

If you are a small business, it is certainly appropriate to pitch free product or discounts to an influence prospect. If you are able to, you can also offer a pay-for-performance arrangement, where for every sale they drive, they earn a commission. This may require the use of affiliate or referral software or attribution tracking by you or your website, but it helps incentivize their involvement without a large cash investment.

Sophisticated influence partners will likely anticipate the size of your budget, so they won't be offended if you don't have a lot of cash to spare. But they won't likely promote you as a favor, either.

The larger your business, the more likely it is you'll need to pay cash to your partners. Many influence prospects have rate sheets or will give you a cost estimate on request. I've engaged dozens of micro-influence partners (between 2,000 and 100,000 online followers) for less than $15,000 for one program. (It involved a charity angle and was community-driven, so it was less commercial in nature.)

I have also managed mega-influence (more than 100,000 followers) campaigns that cost $100,000 and only engaged 10 to 12 individuals. Each influence partner delivered three or four pieces of content as part of those campaigns, which were designed to manufacture more frequency within high-impact influence audiences rather than total reach by lots of influence partners.

I wish there were an easy chart or conversion metric to make budgeting for influence programs easier, but there isn't. Who's the better deal: someone with 100,000 Instagram followers charging $2,500 for one post, or ten people with 15,000 to 30,000 followers who will each do a single post for $250? In the end, it all comes down to how much you have to spend vs. how much effort the influence partner has to put forth, plus how valuable their audience is to your brand.

As you decide how valuable a given influence prospect is to you, add dollar amounts to your list of priority partners and mark those you can stand to lose if your budget is spent by the time you reach them.

PREPARE THE PITCHES

I know you keep thinking, "OK! Let's pitch 'em already!" Hold your horses. Many PR pros of the past at this point would load up a generic pitch into an email template and blast it out to everyone on the list. Then they'd wait hopefully for replies or follow up with a phone call to the dozen or so they really covet. This is part of the reason PR got a bad rap in the early days of social media. Impersonal, mass emails hoping for free coverage didn't sit well with bloggers and social media mavens who didn't even know what public relations pros were. Many of them were crucified online for the practice that I came to affectionately call "spraying and praying."

Blasting any large groups with any message is ineffective. But I recognize that there are some influence marketplaces built entirely around the concept of mass outreach to scale programs. You can load your program requirements, talking points, images, and hashtags, and then say, "Any influence partner willing to do this will be paid $100."

You can probably see why I dislike this approach. If building relationships is the key to long-term influence success, blindly offering anyone money to post your pitch is practically the opposite approach. However, it's a fool's game to have an absolute stance.

A client once had several hundred units of excess product—which retailed at around $1,500 a pop—and wanted my team at Cornett to give them away to influence partners in hopes of driving online reviews and social content. The challenge was they had to get rid of them quickly. So we researched and compiled a list of 150 people, dumped them into an email template that allowed us to personalize the name, and sent out the offers all at once.

It wasn't ideal, but we still scored dozens of online reviews and social posts singing the praises of our client's product. And we didn't have to spend a dime beyond the cost of the product. (It helps bolster your nonexistent budget when the product you can provide is fairly valuable.)

If you decide to reach out to a lot of influence targets at once, be very careful. If the email is going to more than a couple of dozen people, you should probably use some sort of email marketing software. But doing so requires that you take several legal steps to comply with the CAN-SPAM Act. Using an email platform also subjects your emails to spam filters. The recipients are also more likely to think your email is just another marketing blast, so they may delete it without even reading.

All these additional steps push your influence targets farther away from a direct, one-on-one relationship with you. It isn't wrong to use them. It is only less preferred.

In ideal situations, you can take the time to prepare your pitches and customize them to each influence prospect. Remember that some will want your pitch to be emailed. Others may ask for direct messages on Twitter or Instagram. Still more may not indicate a preference.

Regardless, all will be more apt to respond if your outreach is relevant to them. Which means you have to customize your pitch, one by one.

That doesn't mean you can't use a template. Whether you email, text, DM, or call on the phone, build a concise script you can leverage. This helps you keep the ask short and sweet, focused, and impactful. One of the worst responses you can get from a prospective influence partner is "TLDR." (Too long; didn't read.)

The Goal of a Pitch Is a Response

The fundamental outcome you want from your pitch is a response. So your template needs to be tight. Tell them who you are, what you're working to build, what the broad ask is, and then lay the golden phrase on them. In my experience, the more direct and concise you are, the better. Anything that beats around the bush or drags on too long makes it less likely they'll respond.

Here's a good example:

Hello, Joe. I'm putting together a private tour at the Stearns & Foster mattress factory for folks who can help us get the word out about a line extension they are launching. Are you interested?

All Joe has to do is say "yes" or "no." I haven't wasted his time. He clearly understands who I am (someone working with Stearns & Foster), what I'm asking for (getting the word out about the new line extension), and how he benefits (gets to come for a private tour to see it made). The details of how much, if anything, we would be willing to pay for his time or his posts and the context of what "getting the word out" means can be saved for a follow-up message. Get them on the hook first and then worry about the specifics.

Now, brevity is my favorite approach, but it's not the only approach. Another way to formulate an initial outreach piece is to make a relevant connection, to hook them into reading a lengthier piece. For example, I often look for a mutual connection or chat with someone who knows them before I reach out. Then I can personalize the pitch in a way that gets their attention.

Take a look at this template version in Figure 9–1 on page 128, which you're welcome to use:

This particular template is useful to deploy when an influence partner you're already working with recommends an influential friend to you.

Of course, both previous examples imply you will need a second pitch template: the detailed follow-up. Having pre-written templates with detailed lists of what your brand is asking for and what the partner will receive in return makes getting to the agreement faster. Since you won't use it until the influence partner says they're interested, at that point you're free to send something with more detail and length.

These templates—which you personalize on each send—help you move more rapidly through the process. Resource documents that outline the nuts and bolts of the program also help you answer each influence partner's questions and concerns faster.

Ultimately, being prepared with these templates helps you avoid ever having to reply to a question with "I'll get back to you on that." That could make the difference between a "Yes" and a "No" from your prospective partner.

EXAMPLES OF A GOOD PITCH

In my years of pitching influence prospects, as well as traditional media, I've had the most success with short, to-the-point messages that simply ask

Hi [Name]!

I'm **[your name]** from **[company]**. I work with **[mutual connection]**, who mentioned that you **[what mutual connection said about the influencer]**.

[Mutual connection] said that it would be a good idea to get in touch with you to learn more about **[topic]** and work on **[project]** together.

Does this sound like something that you would be interested in? If so, I would love to call you some day this week around noon and figure out a way to make it mutually beneficial.

Let me know what you think!

Best,

[Your name]

figure 9-1. The Mutual Connection Template

if the person is interested in knowing more. If they say "yes," that gives me permission to follow up with more details.

Here's an example of an actual pitch I sent to an influence prospect (see Figure 9–2 on page 129). I've changed the name and project details, but the rest is verbatim copy/pasted from my email.

figure 9-2. The Interested? Pitch

Granted, if you have a $3,000 anything to give to your prospective influence partners, it's easy to get people to respond. So that particular effort may have been weighted in my favor. As it happens, it was and the individual I sent this to responded positively and wound up partnering with the client.

But I've also sent emails like this to influence partners I've previously built relationships with (see Figure 9–3 below).

The more familiar you are with them and they with you, the less formal your initial pitch can be. As you might imagine, this one happens to work with good frequency.

In reality, though, you may want to include some more details. Here's another example in Figure 9–4 on page 131 that was a 100 percent cold

**JASON FALLS
to DUDE** ▼

Hey Dude!

Can I send you a couple of bottles of bourbon to come to a product launch and write about it on your blog? Happy to hook you up! LMK!

Falls

figure 9-3. The Friend Pitch

Hello Thomas,

I'm working on a project with ACME Technologies and we are hoping to see if a brief engagement with Mary Smith is possible.

The brand is launching a new waterproof bluetooth speaker for outdoor spaces (it won best new product at CES last year). We've identified Mary as the perfect influencer to help us get the word out about the product since she spends so much of her time in her garden and patio area for her videos.

We were thinking we could send her a unit in exchange for a video review and feature explanation on an upcoming show, then a devoted Facebook and Instagram post with links to an order form customized for her audience.

I have a limited budget, but we can do up to a 15% discount code for her audience. Can you give me an idea of what that might look like in terms of what you need to make this happen?

Thanks so much for the consideration. Here's hoping!

Jason

figure 9-4. The More Details Pitch

email I sent to the talent agent for an influence prospect with more than 2 million followers. Again, I've changed the project details and name, but the rest is verbatim.

In this example, I included a few details about the campaign, but I still kept the pitch straight and to the point. I also didn't try to sell the product or project too much. I can always incorporate more details in the follow-up. Notice that I also recognized the product alone wasn't going to be enough. When an influence prospect has an agent, money will have to change hands or the agent won't get paid. This pitch led to a nice negotiation, so it worked to start the conversation. In the end, however, the manager insisted upon the full fee the influence prospect demanded, which wasn't the best investment for the client.

WHAT HAPPENS WHEN THEY DON'T RESPOND?

While there have been 23 official perfect games in Major League Baseball history, there really is no such thing as a perfect game when you're pitching members of the media or influence prospects. Sure, you might have a one-off effort: send one email to one person who says yes, and then you're batting a thousand. But the reality is that when you pitch ideas, you're lucky to get a 50 percent response rate.

This doesn't mean you've failed. The average news producer, editor, reporter, or online influencer probably receives hundreds of emails per week. A good percentage of those emails are from people asking for their time and attention on topics that are of little relevance or interest to them.

Truthfully, your target person of influence often doesn't read your pitch at all. Other times they read it, but they don't immediately find it relevant or have time to pursue it. And, yes, sometimes it never gets where it's supposed to go: it gets caught in spam filters, you have the wrong email address, the person you targeted no longer works there, and so on.

We've already talked about what you can do to break through that clutter and be more relevant with our tips on brevity, using the golden phrase, and catching their attention. It's worth repeating, though, that your best tactic to get a response is to tailor your topic, content, or opportunity to make it highly relevant to them and their audience.

Even then, you may get crickets chirping in response. My rule of thumb is to send one pitch and one follow-up. If I don't get a response after that, they aren't interested, and I move on. As someone who receives a fair number of pitches myself as an influential person in the digital marketing space, I can tell you anything beyond one follow-up can become annoying. In a few rare circumstances, when the influence prospect is just too perfect to pass up, I've sent one more follow-up, normally very short, just to say, "I won't bother you again, but I wanted to check one last time if you'd be interested in this." But two messages is generally my limit when I'm trying to get someone's attention.

Just remember that if you don't get a response, it's not personal. Some of your influence targets have plenty to do every day without having to sort through dozens or even hundreds of emails from marketers pitching them on ideas or fans asking for one thing or another.

But if you do get that response and your influence prospect shows interest in your proposal, you are now ready for Part III of this book. It's time to deploy Winfluence in action.

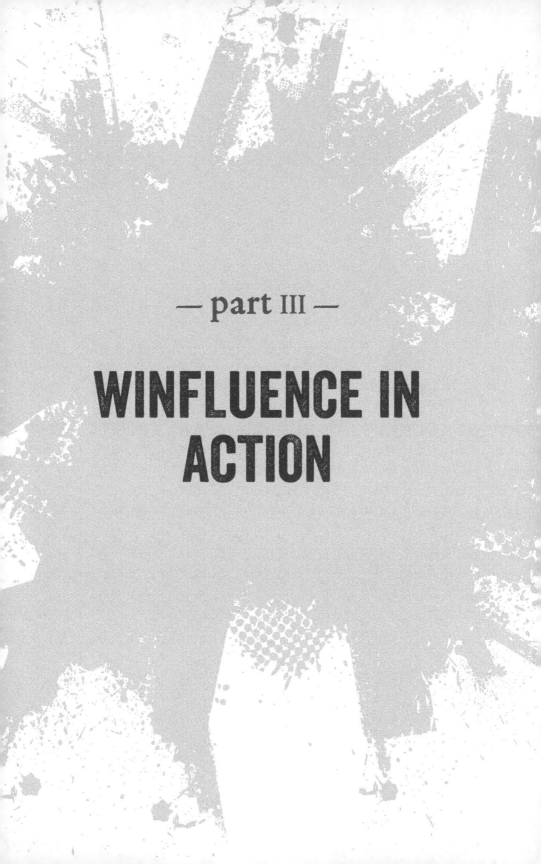

— part III —

WINFLUENCE IN ACTION

THE FOUR PURPOSES OF INFLUENCE

U p to now, we've talked a lot about who wields influence, how to find them, and the practical and tactical methods of employing influence marketing for your business or brand. We've touched on the strategic side of influence marketing in terms of meeting your goals and objectives. There's even been a bit of discussion on how to measure the success of your influence programs, though we'll talk about that even more in Chapter 15.

One topic we have yet to really flesh out is the purpose of your influence marketing. Driving sales or brand awareness are the practical results of your purpose, but they aren't really the purpose itself.

What is the definition of a purpose? It is the *reason for being*. That's more significant than whatever KPI or metric you're trying to achieve.

In this chapter, you'll learn influence marketing's four reasons for being and see how they connect to advertising, public relations, ratings and reviews, and word-of-mouth marketing.

INFLUENCE MARKETING'S REASONS FOR BEING

Depending on which college textbook you look in, there are between five and ten methods, or modes, of marketing communication. In general, they boil down to advertising, sales, public relations, customer service (which I translate to ratings and reviews, the voice of the customer online), and word of mouth. Some lists also add direct or sales force (which are just part of sales, in my opinion) and offer event, digital marketing, or other subdivisions as modes of their own. Others leave off customer service or word of mouth as if they fit into one of the other modes.

The four reasons a company or brand might engage a person with influence align with four of the major modes of marketing communications. These reasons for being are:

1. to persuade (aligns with advertising)
2. to associate (aligns with public relations)
3. to validate (aligns with ratings and reviews)
4. to enthuse (aligns with word of mouth)

Take a look at Figure 10–1 on page 139 to see how these align.

In the next four chapters, we'll not only dive deeper into each of these purposes but also illustrate how they come to life in businesses and brands like yours. But let's define each before we dissect their how and why.

Employing Advertising Influence (Persuade)

The default purpose of most influence marketing programs is to advertise a product or service. In fact, most of the influence marketing examples

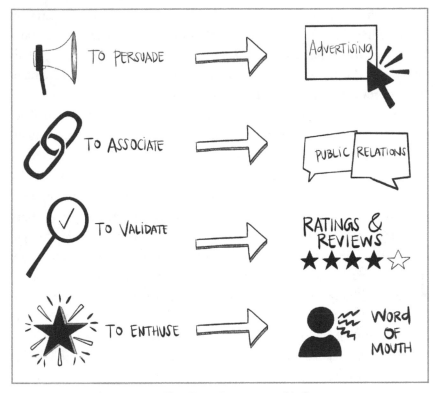

figure 10–1. The Four Purposes of Influence

you've seen are likely efforts to persuade the audience to try or buy a given product or service.

Leveraging influence partners as an advertising mechanism focuses their efforts on driving brand awareness to increase the likelihood of consideration or trial. Or they will offer an overt call to action to purchase or try the product.

This type of influence marketing dates back centuries. In 1765, Josiah Wedgwood had developed a more refined, cream-colored earthenware at his factory at Burslem. His work caught the attention of Queen Charlotte, who commissioned him to make a tea set. The enterprising Wedgwood called his new line "Queen's Ware," and the local newspaper announced he had been appointed "potter to the queen."

By the time he died 30 years later, his pottery was popular worldwide. He was worth the equivalent of hundreds of millions of dollars in today's measures.

The difference between having a reigning monarch in the days of British imperialism endorse your work and, let's say, having a fashion influence partner on Instagram wear your designer outfit in a post is substantial. But the activation is similar. You leverage their endorsement of your product, service, or brand to encourage others to buy it.

On the B2B side of the aisle, an influence partner may be used to persuade people to sign up for an email list or download a piece of content in exchange for their contact information. That lead is the B2B version of a B2C sale. It's not a $49 pair of sunglasses or shoes, but that just might be what you have to pay per lead to convert one sale of $49,000 or more.

Software companies are the best at using influence marketing in the B2B space. Most of them use webinars and white papers to lure prospects to sign up, handing over their email address or other contact information to do so and becoming a lead in their funnel. Sprinklr, an enterprise social media marketing solution set, leveraged communications guru Peter Shankman for a crisis communications webinar in 2019. Not only did the software company put significant social media and paid media resources into promoting the webinar, but Shankman promoted it to his audience as well.

This technique is how hundreds of technology companies have built a lead pipeline over the years. It is a content marketing-era version of advertising—instead of buying an ad in a trade magazine or even on a trade industry website, you put that advertising spend behind an influence partner to promote the webinar and your company to their audience. You also lay out advertising dollars along other channels to promote the webinar and the influence partner's involvement with your company for maximum effectiveness.

The focal point of the persuasion in an advertising campaign may be to convince people to try or buy a product, but it may also be to convince them to think differently about a company or a brand. In this connotation, you might easily confuse the activity with public relations. But, as you'll see below, persuading someone to think differently is still persuasion, not association.

Employing Public Relations Influence (Associate)

A softer purpose sometimes employed by brands in leveraging influence partners is that of association. Public relations, in many ways, is focused not on a specific persuasive direction—trying to convince an audience to do or think something—but merely on associating a product, service, company, or issue with another in order to borrow trust or equity from them.

In other words, the Tom James Co. may work through public relations channels to get *Esquire* to feature their latest suit designs, but their goal isn't for *Esquire* to tell people to buy custom clothing from Tom James. It's more about simply associating the clothier with *Esquire*. The brand equity transferred by association elevates the Tom James Co. in the mind of the reader.

This technique is often employed in more long-term relationships, where the influence partner is using the product but not openly asking people to buy it. Or when they talk about the social issues or nonproduct aspects of a brand or company to further associate the brand with their stance on the issue.

A strong example of this is the relationship Dove Men+Care has with many bloggers, podcasters, and those influential in the dad and fatherhood space. The men's personal care brand from Unilever regularly sponsors events like the Dad 2.0 Summit in order to connect and partner with fathers. It works to amplify advocacy for passing paid family medical leave legislation and including paternity leave in that legislation.

"Unilever and Dove Men+Care, part of the larger Dove family, are so committed to finding purpose within their brands," Jordan Lewis, brand manager at Unilever U.S. for Dove Men+Care, said. "[They are committed] to finding sustainability, both environmentally and socially. That is one of the most incredible things about the Dove portfolio, is that they are highly driven by their purpose. For Dove Men+Care, that has always been expanding and creating opportunities for men to show care."

So Dove Men+Care influence engagements may mention the brand, but they are focused on associating it with social advocacy that supports its core audience of men, many of whom are fathers.

In a B2B context, we can go back to the example of Shankman and Sprinklr, but think of their association as more of an investment over time. IBM created fantastic awareness of its Watson computer by challenging *Jeopardy!* champions Brad Rutter and Ken Jennings in 2011. The computer, designed to understand natural human speech, beat both humans to win a $1 million prize, and overnight nearly everyone in America suddenly knew what IBM's Watson was.

But they didn't know how to leverage the publicity, so IBM's Watson marketing team decided to engage people with influence to solve the problem. It invited 24 notable speakers, authors, bloggers, and analysts in the enterprise software, technology, and marketing space to join a new program called the Futurists.

These futurists were not just treated as sponsored content outlets or product endorsers, however. They were invited to IBM events, asked to contribute content to IBM's blog, and engaged to host webinars and contribute to white papers.

The Watson marketing team wasn't leveraging them for advertising calls to action or lead generation. They wanted to build a relationship and association with these influential people over time. In that relationship, they were pushing some advertising levers, with webinars and the like, but the central point was to ensure that these notable people, whom enterprise software purchasers looked to for advice, were telling the story of Watson and its applications to companies.

The first year of the IBM Futurists program was so successful that they expanded and invited me to be a part of the group. I was compensated at a modest level to write blog posts for their website about social listening, which included explaining how Watson's marketing engine can make the process of analyzing millions of data points in social conversations quicker and more efficiently than other platforms. They also flew me to a couple of conferences to speak, live tweet, and report for both their channels and mine.

At no point was I ever asked to sell Watson. None of us were. We were simply there to associate ourselves with a big company and a new product that other companies could use.

Employing Ratings & Reviews Influence (Validate)

If expert reviews are one of the fundamental triggers that push consumers to buy a product, and we can agree that influential people are viewed as experts, then leveraging your influence partners to recommend your product or service should be their primary function. There are two things that snag the thinking of most marketers here.

First, this is another area where our bastardization of the term "influencer" distorts our thinking. An "influencer," we believe, is someone who takes a selfie while wearing your makeup or hat or watch. They don't do useful things like link to your website or post a rating or review of your product on your website. Or someone else's website.

And that begets the second snag. Many sites that host customer reviews have policies against incentivizing or paying people to review your product or service. Marketers, especially SEO types, thus keep a big, strong wall between the two practices.

But product reviews hosted on your website—and thus curated by you—are still fundamentally critical data points for search engines. And places like Facebook treat reviews like posts—as long as you abide by the community ethics standards, and the Federal Trade Commission's (FTC) guidance on disclosures, it should be fine to ask people to post reviews.

And your influence partners will do so if you ask.

An influence partner campaign my team at Cornett ran for Tempur-Pedic's LuxeAdapt mattress not only asked them to post on social networks but also leave a review on the Tempur-Pedic website, where the company aggregates reviews from various places. Our influence agreement clarified the nature of that review:

> — "Talent will post at least one (1) honest, FTC-compliant review of the mattress on TempurPedic.com with the influencer's legal name, city of residence, etc." —

That program engaged 50 influence partners in the weeks following the LuxeAdapt's release into the market, helping to seed qualified reviews for website visitors to consider.

We'll look deeper into the ethics of influence review strategies in Chapter 13. In no way would I recommend violating a review or social networking site's terms of service, not to mention your own sound ethics, to cheat the system. But there's nothing wrong with encouraging people to review your product or service as long as you are directing them to give honest reviews, not just positive ones.

To truly integrate influence marketing across disciplines and lift your brand, you have to think beyond your initial instincts and focus on awareness. Ratings and reviews are critical to your buyers' decision-making process.

"The Millennial Consumer Study," a 2015 survey of Millennials by Elite Daily and Millennial Branding, found that only 1 percent of Millennials trust advertising, while 33 percent rely largely on blog reviews before making purchases. If that isn't a motivation to use your influence partners to drive online reviews, you won't find a better one.

Employing Word-of-Mouth Influence (Enthuse)

The final, and perhaps most important, purpose of influence marketing takes a bit from each of the others but is distinctive in that it doesn't have to persuade, associate, or drive reviews. It is the art of using influential people to drive word-of-mouth marketing for your brand.

Yes, you can use word of mouth to get people to try or buy your product. In that regard, it functions like advertising. You can use it to associate your brand with a given influence partner, cause, or conversation, so it also functions like public relations. And leveraging word of mouth to drive reviews is almost a tactical execution of the purpose to drive recommendations.

But expertly executed word of mouth does all of them. It builds not just customers, but loyal customers. It drives not just online reviews, but genuine, proactive recommendations from one person to another. Someone saying "You have to try this!" in a conversation is infinitely more powerful than clicking on a star rating on Amazon or Google.

Dettol is the bestselling antiseptic cleaner in the world, but in 2011 it found itself lagging in third place in the biggest opportunity market: China. When surveys showed it was largely used just to clean floors, and not all the other surfaces it was intended for, the British company launched a convenient, hand-held spray bottle version of the cleaner.

It then sent the spray bottles to 4,000 influential Chinese moms whose online content indicated a passion for household care. (Remember, China is a market of more than 1 billion people, so 4,000 is just a drop in the bucket.) The instructions were to try it but also pass along bottles to their friends. The brilliant technique of seeding product with influence partners who could then immediately influence their circles of people blew the campaign wide open.

Dettol's brand awareness numbers jumped 500 percent, purchase intent doubled, and sales increased 86 percent. The estimates from its agency, Singapore-based firm Advocaci, are that the campaign reached 46 percent of its intended target audience.

Chapter 14 will drill deeper into how influence partners can be engaged not just to add to your word-of-mouth marketing programs but to serve as the keystone for the efforts. After all, you want WOMM to come from expert, credible, and trusted sources. And who do prospective customers trust more than the influential people they already rely on for content, advice, and recommendations?

WHAT THE PURPOSES MEAN FOR YOU

When I have doubts, confusion, or just get caught up in the details of a client project, I always re-center myself by asking "Why?" Why are we doing this? Why is the brand using this advertising? Why are they paying for our time? Why are they leveraging influence partners?

The purpose—the *reason for being*—is the simple answer to the question. If that answer is that they are trying to persuade, I instantly know we should focus on making people try or buy a product, or perhaps think differently about the company or issue. If the answer is to associate with a given mindset, issue, or influence partner, I know we must deploy more relationship-building techniques aligned with PR to produce a positive association in the consumer's mind.

If the answer to "Why?" is to validate the value our product or service provides, I immediately know producing reviews is the output we're looking for. And if the answer is to build passion around what the client has or is, I know we're combining any or all of those to produce word of mouth driven through or by influential people.

These four *reasons for being* are your purpose. Your goals get closer to ground level, but not as close as your objectives or tactics. I find it easier to express your purpose for using influence marketing in singular terms.

Why are you using influence? To . . .

* persuade
* associate
* validate
* enthuse

Let's look at each in greater detail and see how brands are paving their way to influence marketing success.

11

EMPLOYING ADVERTISING INFLUENCE (PERSUADE)

Using influential partners for advertising purposes—to persuade an audience to try or buy
a product or service, or perhaps to think differently about something—is the simplest and most
common form of influence marketing, at least in the
context of leveraging online influencers.

Say a brand wants to reach women who love to
cook and travel, so they partner with Candace Sampson
(@lifeinpleasantville). The traditional method is to buy

an ad on her blog (lifeinpleasantville.com). The influence marketing method is to negotiate a fee for her to incorporate the brand into her normal content in a way that delivers a genuine recommendation to buy or try the product.

That approach can scale quite well as long as you can identify a large group of online influencers who reach the audience you're looking for and have a big enough budget to pay for it. Many influence marketing agencies and software platforms are constructed with this in mind.

In this chapter, I'm going to share five case studies of advertising influence in action. I'll illustrate how each of these is an example of Winfluence and give you inspiration to build your own successful campaigns.

EXPRESS DRIVES SALES, EFFICIENCY

Retail clothing brand Express expanded its loyalty and influence program in 2018 by including influence partners and even employees in a campaign designed to drive more in-store and online sales. Using Mavrck, an influence marketing platform, Express identified both macro- and micro-influence partners it wanted to participate.

The brand gave influence partners and employee participants unique discount codes to share with their social audiences. It paid those partners with larger audiences who required fees but got many micro-influence partners to participate for cash rewards or points in the Express Ambassador program, which could be used for product. The theme of the campaign was to have each participant design their own style choices for work attire, using the hashtag #ExpressYourRules.

With unboxing videos, fashion photographs, and enthusiastic recommendations to shop and buy at Express, the campaign used people of influence at all levels—macro-influence partners, micro-influence partners, and employees with audiences of varying sizes.

The brand put paid spend behind some influence posts and cross-posted many of them on its own channels to amplify the unique content and ideas coming from campaign participants. That produced a 33 percent increase in engagement rates for macro-influence partners and an eye-popping 134 percent jump for those of the micro-influence size. The micro-influence network for the brand grew almost 12 percent because of the campaign as well.

The unique codes given to each partner worked in-store or online and were tracked throughout the campaign. As a result, not only could Express track the results of their influence marketing spend, they could pinpoint exactly how much revenue came from each individual partner. The efficiency improvements in their influence marketing methods alone likely make the campaign worth the investment.

But here's the real goods: The campaign drove sales.

While specific numbers are seldom shared in case studies like this, Express and Mavrck did share that the campaign drove a 168 percent ROI for the company. Let's say they spent $500,000 on the campaign. That would mean the company made $840,000 in revenue. That may not be as effective as, say, a TV ad campaign or even a direct-mail piece. But the efficiency created by knowing which influence partners drive the best revenue margins could make the next campaign's returns exceed 200 or 300 percent.

That's before you get into the soft metrics like impressions (15 percent more on Instagram for this campaign), awareness, relationships developed, and other data points. For example, Express learned that this campaign drove more than three-fourths of its audience to buy in-store, not online. In an era of retail evaporation, that could be a useful insight.

THE ONLINE/OFF-LINE SUCCESS HYBRID

Selling products in your own stores is one challenge. Selling your product in an established retail partner's stores is another, but if you manage it, it can unlock tremendous growth for a brand. MiaMily found itself faced with this monumental challenge—and opportunity—in 2018.

The company's ergonomically designed baby carrier takes pressure off the parent's back and joints while helping to prevent hip dysplasia in children. The brand pitched its carrier to Buy Buy Baby, a popular online and off-line retailer for parents. That company's beta test with new products is to offer them online first. If they sell well there, they include them in retail inventory as well.

MiaMily seized the opportunity. It engaged influential parenting content creators to try the carrier and post personal, authentic stories that related to the everyday lives of the influence partners' audience. The blog posts and videos were then amplified by social shares but also scored for clickthrough rates to BuyBuyBaby.com's sales page by influence marketing firm Carusele. The ones that scored well with conversions were amplified further with a supplemental paid spend.

The coordinated effort pushed a brand-directed influx of traffic to BuyBuyBaby.com, exceeding their click goal by 159 percent. The brand saw an 84 percent sales lift online, which helped convince Buy Buy Baby to carry the product in its retail locations. While the company wouldn't share specific sales numbers, offering a product in 135 stores across the United States and Canada probably added more than a little to their bottom line.

ONE INFLUENCE PARTNER, INCREASED SALES

Few influence marketing case studies excite me more than Martin Bamford's. The financial planner based in Surrey, U.K., carved out a nice name for himself first as a blogger, then as a book author, and then as a podcaster.

In an industry where trust and credibility are at a premium, Bamford built his thought leadership platform over the course of a 17-year career at Informed Choice, an independent financial planning firm. He started blogging there in 2003. That long tie to an accredited business gave his blog readers and social media followers a level of trust in Bamford's ideas.

The reason his influence platform is so remarkable, though, is that it doesn't boast big, sexy "influence marketing" numbers. Informed Choice has a popular blog (icfp.co.uk/resources/blog/) and podcast (*Informed Choice Radio*) driven mostly by Bamford. But his social platforms consist of a standard LinkedIn profile (which only displays 500+ followers publicly) and 11,000 or so followers on Twitter. He has just over 700 followers on Instagram. And his YouTube channel, if you can call it that, had just ten subscribers the last time I checked.

Search for Martin Bamford in most influence marketing software, and you won't find much. (That will change once these platforms begin to incorporate more impact metrics around podcasts and blogs, but as of early 2020, they simply don't pay attention to them.) He told me his podcast gets a couple of thousand downloads per episode; in total, it has passed 350,000 downloads since it began in 2014.

Global investment bank UBS, however, cherished Bamford's audience, who look to him for financial planning advice. Onalytica's analysis of the people whom high-net-worth individuals trust for financial advice in Britain came back with Martin Bamford at or near the top of the list. It wasn't about the size of Bamford's audience but the quality. These were exactly the kind of people UBS wanted to reach.

So they reached out to Bamford and pitched Nick Tucker, UBS's head of wealth management, as a guest on the podcast. His focus was to help Bamford's audience understand more about leaving wealth to your heirs and suggest UBS's own content, including white paper-type lead-generation efforts, as resources.

This single appearance by a company representative on an influential person's podcast produced nearly four times as many leads as UBS's reports had previously. Even at a modest conversion rate, a new lead that purchases a $100,000 annuity is worth thousands of dollars to the brand.

ONE MORE INFLUENCE PARTNER, INCREASED SALES

Carphone Warehouse is sort of like the Best Buy for mobile devices in Britain. In 2017, as it prepared for the Samsung Galaxy S8 launch, the company looked for creative ideas to reach mainstream, non-tech-focused, Millennial/Gen Z audiences. If they could reach beyond the early tech adopters, it would vault sales of the new phone and its fancy features beyond expectations.

While phone reviews are useful, consumer interest in searching for phone reviews had been steadily declining. As a result, the brand and its influence firm, 1000heads, turned to an unlikely "reviewer" to break through the noise.

Elijah Quashie is a fried chicken fanatic. He is known, in fact, as The Chicken Connoisseur in England. His YouTube channel, The Pengest Munch, launched in 2015 and now boasts more than 700,000 subscribers. His content is essentially fun and witty reviews of fried chicken restaurants in London. As cheeky as it sounds, Carphone Warehouse knew a carefully executed partnership would get the Galaxy S8 in front of the right audience.

The resulting video was Quashie showing the counter clerk at New Jersey Chicken in Colindale, London, all the phone's features. He showed the iris scanning feature to unlock, the size of the screen, and beautiful images taken with its 12-megapixel camera. He even tested the phone's waterproof ability by squirting ketchup and mayonnaise on it and then rinsing it off.

For his audience, the video was interesting, useful, and in step with the type of content they expect from his channel. It was released on both Quashie's and Carphone Warehouse's social channels. Targeted paid ads were then deployed on Facebook to drive further awareness among the target audience. The video was even used in TV commercials on Britain's Channel 4 On Demand, further promoting the launch.

Did the video do its job and persuade? It most certainly did. The video amassed more than 2.5 million views in the course of the campaign; drove almost 60,000 reactions, comments, and shares; and helped drive a 43 percent higher level of preorders for the Galaxy 8 than for the S7, which was released the previous year.

An excellent influence effort like the Carphone Warehouse campaign really serves as a hybrid of multiple reasons for being. The video created an experience in Quashie's review of the phone, persuaded people to preorder and buy it, and associated the product with a hip, trendy content creator like Quashie, whose style sparked the passion behind word-of-mouth referrals.

Because if you were a fan of The Chicken Connoisseur and saw that review, you were going to mention it to more than one person.

THE BEAUTY OF A $1 BILLION INFLUENCE BUDGET

If one influence partner like Quashie, or even Martin Bamford, can be that effective, imagine what hundreds of them can do. While the chicken or financial services spaces are far different animals than the beauty space, Estée Lauder spends 75 percent of its marketing budget on digital, with the vast majority of that earmarked for influence marketing.

"Seventy-five percent of our investments now are in digital social media influencers, and they're revealing to be highly productive," CEO Fabrizio Freda said in the company's fourth-quarter earnings call in 2019. He cited online influencer partners' ability to consistently communicate a product's quality to a target audience as the reason his brands like them for growth.

Estée Lauder owns a few dozen skin-care, hair, and makeup brands, so that investment is spread out over multiple budgets, but the company reported quarterly net sales of almost $15 billion on that same quarterly call, a 9 percent increase from the previous year. Most of the company's brands leverage influential creators for brand awareness campaigns, but some have begun including shoppable posts which drive fans to direct points of purchase.

Case studies from their individual brands vary, but when a publicly traded company plants its flag in a marketing method to the tune of ten figures, you'd better believe the end result is increased sales and revenue. Previous reports showed that Estée Lauder spent $900 million on influence marketing in 2017, so assuming their budget has now topped $1 billion isn't a stretch.

PERSUASION IS THE NEW TREND

All the examples in this chapter are influence programs that employed advertising influence. They persuaded an audience to try or buy a product. Being persuasive is truly at the core of successful advertising and marketing. What more are we trying to do, in a general sense, than persuade an audience to buy a product, try a service, or change their mind or behavior?

Jim Joseph, author of the book *The Conscious Marketer*, wrote that being persuasive should be the goal of marketing campaigns.

"To be a Conscious Marketer, brands need to be more persuasive in their messaging to convince people of the value they offer," he wrote. "It's the only way to stand out. It's not just about sending out messages or getting others to share them but it's about getting consumers to embody them . . . to take them on and to insert the brand into their lives. The only way for a brand to do that is to be persuasive."

Remember Robert Cialdini's six principles of influence, which we discussed in Chapter 3? They came from his seminal book *Influence: The Psychology of Persuasion*. One can argue the terms *influence* and *persuasion* are somewhat interchangeable. If you persuade someone, you have influence over them. But if you influence someone, you may not necessarily be using persuasion. You may be using one of the other three reasons for being.

You'll also note the case studies in this chapter didn't mention any off-line people of influence. That's because the execution of advertising influence is typically limited to those who have an overt platform on which to advertise. The local PTA president or union shop boss isn't traditionally used that way. Those off-line influential people are used less for persuasion and more when it comes to association (which we'll discuss in the next chapter).

EMPLOYING PUBLIC RELATIONS INFLUENCE (ASSOCIATION)

I f advertising is more focused on persuasion, public relations can be said to focus on association. These are more subtle influence marketing efforts, in that they simply wish to align the product or brand with the influential person, idea, or cause.

In this chapter, I'll show you five more case studies that use public relations influence, or association. You'll see how successful influence marketing can happen by using just one influential person.

And you'll find more sparks of inspiration to drive your own Winfluence efforts.

Association is akin to awareness. (It actually *is* awareness but with context.) For example, the audience for the Amazon Prime series *Sneaky Pete* sees Marius Josipovic (Giovanni Ribisi's character) celebrate a big score by sharing a bottle of Pappy Van Winkle bourbon with his crew of con artists. That product placement creates awareness for Pappy (as it's known in bourbon circles). But it creates that awareness in the context of being something celebratory and saved for a special occasion.

Since we're talking about awareness and association, as opposed to persuasion, we're veering into the disciplines of public relations, political lobbying, and issues management. But it can also be that a challenger brand is trying to set the stage with association or consideration before hitting the audience hard with persuasive messaging.

For example, the thought of selling a computer mainframe to businesses in 2014 was ludicrous. The era of cloud computing was upon us, so those old, antiquated systems were destined for postmodern art projects. But IBM knew the concept of a mainframe was misunderstood. All computers connect to mainframes on a daily basis. They're not outdated; they're a necessity.

But, as TopRank Blog's Ashley Zeckman reported in 2015, IBM couldn't just come up with some new persuasive ad that would sell mainframes. Instead, they asked some of their largest clients, companies like Walmart and Visa, to tell stories about how IBM's mainframes have helped their businesses. These client-led stories became a consideration campaign called "The Engines of Progress." Zeckman wrote: "[W]hat you'll notice is that IBM leverages modern themes throughout this entire campaign and that they aren't pushing their product . . . These videos helped tell IBM's story digitally and the clients saw this as an association with something very iconic to be proud of."

Once the foundation of consideration was laid, IBM could shift its messaging to a more persuasive context. And in case you didn't catch it, the "influencers" in this case study were IBM's customers telling their story. These companies were representative of the "People Like Me" IBM was trying to reach.

ASSOCIATING A BRAND WITH A LIFESTYLE

Buffalo Trace Bourbon is the namesake gem of the family of bourbons produced at the Buffalo Trace Distillery in Frankfort, Kentucky. The brand is built around the idea that the mighty buffalo carved paths across the wilderness that led pioneers across the country. That pioneering, independent spirit carries forward in the brand, which is positioned for those who #StandStrong.

The bourbon and distillery are clients of Cornett, the agency where I work, so I have the great pleasure of working with such an iconic bourbon brand.

Buffalo Trace has always had more of a word-of-mouth approach to marketing. It invests in social media content and engagement, and thus influence marketing, as one of its primary approaches to consumers. In 2018, we worked together to take Buffalo Trace's influence programs to a different level.

One influence partner the brand worked with on some sponsored posts was Derek Wolf (@overthefirecooking). His outdoor grilling content had helped him build a large Instagram audience of mostly men in their 20s and 30s who enjoyed the outdoors, working with their hands, and cooking delicious meals over fires—all qualities that, if stated differently, sounded a lot like *pioneering* and *independent*. Wolf's fans would certainly #StandStrong.

After executing a couple of sponsored Instagram posts, the brand team saw the engagement was high and Wolf's audience responded well to the partnership. It thus set about to deepen that association and help bake Buffalo Trace into the Over the Fire experience.

In February 2019, Over the Fire Cooking and Buffalo Trace debuted a video series on Facebook, YouTube, and Instagram called "Over the Fire Cooking." Instead of his usual time-lapse, 60-second cooking videos, Wolf presented 4- to 5-minute episodes where he showed more of the preparation and cooking process. It was a cooking-show approach that put Wolf front and center as the star of the show, giving him an enhanced online presence.

But then Buffalo Trace did something very smart. Instead of just having Wolf host the show and demonstrate how to cook various meals, it invited a guest (with online influence) on each episode to help tell a complete narrative through the season. Episode one featured Danielle Prewett (@wildandwhole), a wild-game hunter who talked about the health aspects and challenge of hunting your meat. Episode two saw Wolf visit Porter Road Butcher in Nashville (@porterroad), where owner Chris Carter showed how to break down an animal and prepare it for cooking. In the third installment, Jared Thatcher (@boothillblades) and Wolf forged a knife blade and talked about the importance of cutlery in meal preparation. The four-episode miniseries ended with Wolf cooking alongside Buffalo Trace Distillery's master distiller, Harlen Wheatley, and then reuniting with the three other influential guests for a celebratory dinner at the distillery.

Of course, each episode ended with the guests raising a glass of Buffalo Trace Bourbon to a meal well done.

That alignment leads consumers to keep a given brand top of mind when purchasing. Buffalo Trace's influence program wasn't focused on driving direct sales. It was working to associate the brand with the consumers' interests and lifestyle. It was relationship influence.

SPEND MARKETING DOLLARS TODAY, MEASURE SUCCESS IN 2040

This type of influence becomes even more important when you are faced with spending a marketing budget today that won't be realized in sales for 20 more years. That may be a bit of an exaggeration for most brands, but when your goal is awareness, you're playing the long game.

For luxury brands, particularly those that appeal to an aspirational audience, that 20-year wait might not actually be a stretch. In fact, piano maker Steinway & Sons uses influence marketing expressly to position the brand as aspirational for the 2040 customer, according to a January 2020 article in *The Drum*.

Steinway's senior director of marketing, Anthony Gilroy, explained in the article that the high-end piano brand was once the keyboard du jour of the elite piano set, but public awareness has waned in the past 20 years. The brand is looking out for the next 20 by investing in both celebrity and lifestyle influence partners.

From twentysomething piano virtuoso Tiffany Poon (@tiffanypianist), with 67,000 followers on Instagram plus almost 200,000 subscribers on

YouTube, and New York-based composer Eric Christian von Fricken (@eric christian; 255,000 Instagram followers) to trendy fashion influence partner Jessica Wang (@jessicawang; 734,000 Instagram followers), the piano maker is weaving its brand into premium culture content.

They're not specifically trying to convert direct customers. Steinway pianos range in price, but they go all the way up to seven figures. This influence marketing play is all about association. It wants to appeal to aspiring pianists but also to people with high net worth or those who want to be such—to associate Steinway with a premium, exclusive lifestyle.

More than 60 percent of Jessica Wang's followers are 17 to 24 years old, according to influence marketing platform Julius. Steinway knows a five-figure or six-figure piano may not be affordable for them now. But 20 years from now . . . it might be.

AN INFLUENCE PARTNER WITHOUT INFLUENCE PLATFORMS

Lest we forget, influence is not exclusive to online activities. Eitan Hersh, a political science professor at Tufts University, expertly outlined perhaps the best case study of off-line influence marketing in his 2020 book *Politics Is for Power: How to Move Beyond Political Hobbyism, Take Action, and Make Real Change.* In it, he told the story of Ukrainian-American activist Naakh Vysoky, a retirement home resident in Boston's Brighton neighborhood, who almost single-handedly controlled, via his influence, the votes of 1,000 or so people living in, or connected to, the building.

Vysoky was always known to be active and helpful for his neighbors and friends, but when the 1996 welfare reform law, known as the Personal Responsibility and Work Opportunity Reconciliation Act, was passed, he became a real-life (as opposed to online) influencer. The bill included a clause that denied legal immigrants access to disability and food stamps unless they applied for citizenship. Knowing most of his fellow retirement home residents were legal immigrants but hampered by language, health, and mobility challenges that made the citizenship process very difficult, Vysoky decided to help.

He and his wife, Klara, started study groups, helped the residents learn how to read and write basic English, and coached them through the face-to-face interview questions required to pass. Vysoky also advocated for other legal immigrants by talking to the media, bringing the unfortunate consequences of the bill to light. He was eventually invited to speak at the National Press Club and became the voice of an underserved population.

Soon after, political candidates started coming to Vysoky's housing complex. He organized committees to get the word out about the ones willing to help people like him. He became known as the Ukrainian Boss among politicos. He wielded true influence, and not a bit of it was digital.

Everything about Vysoky's story is public relations. He organized community events and activities to help impacted groups of people. He shared information and took action to help guide them through the intimidating government bureaucracy, and in the process he built trust. With that trust, he then could influence how they thought about issues, policies, and even candidates.

Associating with Vysoky became a smart move for a candidate looking for key votes in Brighton. Doing so meant they also became trusted—and got elected.

ALIGNING A BRAND WITH DEATH

There's loss, as in not associating with Vysoky in Boston and subsequently losing an election, and then there's loss, as in the death of a loved one. Marie Curie understands that second meaning very well. Not the scientist who helped develop the theory of radioactivity, but the nonprofit organization that bears her name in the United Kingdom.

Marie Curie (the organization) provides care for terminally ill people and their families. It has more than 4,000 employees, 11,000 volunteers, and revenues in the hundreds of millions to provide thousands of British people with hospice and similar care.

But to create brand awareness among their target audience of midlife and older individuals—the ones who often have to place parents and loved ones in assisted care—Marie Curie has to force difficult conversations. They need their prospective customers to talk about death, dying, and bereavement, not just that of their loved ones but sometimes of themselves. And that is a tall order.

In early 2019, Marie Curie identified six influential content creators (bloggers, Instagrammers, and YouTubers) whose audiences and topics offered strong opportunities to engage around that subject. They hosted each in meetings at Marie Curie hospices, where the six could learn about the issues that needed to be addressed and where they could capture and create content.

The influence partners shared content around the topics, mentioning Marie Curie frequently as an authority on the subject, over a three-month campaign. Four of them officially signed on to be Marie Curie brand ambassadors at the end of the campaign.

To give you an example of the type of content that was created, one of the influence partners, Kate Davis-Holmes, wrote this in her *Kate on Thin Ice* blog, which focused on an aging female demographic: "Their work is tangible, delivering results and making a real difference to the lives of thousands of families in the U.K. And their work is only set to evolve: changing the conversation about terminal illness to one more positive and less fearful."

This influence program aligned Marie Curie with topics like death and dying, which are ordinarily negative. But it did so in a way that broke down the stigmas associated with broaching them, which is what Marie Curie needed it to do. It aligned the brand with those topics as an authoritative resource and the logical nonprofit organization to support in order to help those dealing with terminal illness and the emotions that accompany it.

While most brands would not want to be associated with death and dying, Marie Curie does. And in Great Britain it is, but with a welcome hug of comfort, rather than backing away in fear.

CHANGING PERCEPTIONS THROUGH INFLUENCE STRATEGIES

What happens when the perception of you in your market or industry doesn't align with what you provide? Associating your brand with what you do becomes of paramount importance. Mitie, a facilities management company in the U.K., found itself in that very pickle not long ago. In fact, the perception of the brand was that of a "mop and bucket" company.

However, Mitie is a tech-savvy facilities management brand that doesn't just offer cleaning supplies and equipment to its customers; it is driven by innovation and bleeding-edge property management approaches.

It engaged Onalytica to analyze and recommend the top 500 influential people on the brand's priority topics in the proptech (property technology) segment. The brand reached out to them, asking for their input on an industry report called "The Connected Workspace: The Digital Transformation of Facilities Management."

Flattered to be quoted as a resource in a thought leadership piece, most of the influence targets gladly participated, offering their insights, quotes, and more for free. The Mitie team kept up "always-on" social relationships with the prospects, engaging with them on social channels before, during, and after the report's release.

It engaged 15 of the influence prospects for events and additional content creation to seed the report in the industry conversation, so that it wasn't completely relying on the ones who were quoted in the report to share it (although those who were quoted were given the links and requests to do so).

The ensuing conversation about the report, its content, and its author—the Mitie brand—shifted the market's perception of Mitie from a "mop and bucket" company to an innovative facilities management brand. Its measures of brand perception, in fact, showed the association with facilities management increased 200 percent. At the same time, the brand's reach increased 15 percent and it saw a 10 percent jump in website traffic.

Associating the Mitie brand with a different perception was critical for this campaign—and it worked. But perhaps just as important was the alignment and association the program produced with the various influence partners who participated. Mitie is now a leading brand in the conversation around productivity and innovation in the proptech space—a far cry from mops and buckets.

IT'S ALL ABOUT (PUBLIC) RELATIONS

It is fair to remind you that public relations influence is closely tied to PR as a practice, but as you can see from some of the case studies in this chapter, the term has a broader context. Association, as opposed to persuasion, is all about alignment. That connection can be thematic, or it can be through actual relationships between you and the person of influence, or you and their audience.

The ultimate payoff for a business that leverages public relations influence is that an audience is more aware of what the brand is *and* what it's supposed to mean to them. It's the difference between Ford reinforcing their brand pillar of quality and telling you to go buy an F-150.

When someone else tells you to go buy an F-150, that falls into our third purpose of influence: sharing an experience that drives reviews.

EMPLOYING RATINGS AND REVIEW INFLUENCE (VALIDATE)

W hen is the last time you shopped for something online, or shopped for something worth more than $100 or so off-line, that you didn't consult a list of reviews for that product? The reviews may have been on the company's website, Amazon, or another retail site, or they may have appeared on a third-party media outlet or blog.

Remember Jay Baer and Daniel Lemin's "Chatter Matters" research from Chapter 2? Online reviews were the fourth most trusted source for product purchase indicators, behind personal experience, brand familiarity, and recommendations from a friend or family member. Expert reviews immediately followed the more general category.

Those two—online reviews and expert reviews—are the top two purchase recommendation resources we marketers can directly impact.

Reviews are so important that Google relies on them for a big portion of its famous search algorithm. Multiple search engine optimization firms have tested what factors go into Google's consideration set for ranking one product page over another. The consensus is that online reviews typically account for somewhere around 15 percent of the algorithm. In fact, online reviews count for more than social media signals and, in most tests, even more than the on-page factors like keywords and titles.

That's why driving reviews that communicate an influential person's personal experience with a product or service is important enough to be called out as a separate purpose of influence marketing.

In this chapter, I'll explain the right and wrong ways to manufacture reviews for your business. You'll learn how to leverage influence partners to supply reviews the right way. And you'll see three more case studies that illustrate how validation can happen with Winfluence programs.

THE RIGHT WAY AND THE WRONG WAY TO MANUFACTURE REVIEWS

The solution to giving Google and other search engines lots of reviews to consider isn't as easy as paying people to go write reviews. Unfortunately, platforms like Google, Yelp, Tripadvisor, and many more assume that a solicited review is tainted or biased.

Yelp, the popular yet controversial business review site, explicitly tells the businesses listed there they will be penalized by appearing lower in search rankings if they are found to be soliciting reviews. However, the site itself has been accused multiple times over the years of stacking negative reviews on businesses' pages in order to force them to buy ads to "fix" the issue. Yelp has denied the claims.

So if you're following the reasoning here, a business can't solicit reviews, but they can bribe their way into making sure good ones are prioritized? Ironically, Yelp provides the businesses it discourages from soliciting reviews with window stickers and counter signs that—you guessed it—encourage customers to review the business on Yelp. But that's another discussion for another book.

There are actually two types of reviews, and different sites handle them in different ways. There are natural, organic reviews that any customer can write. The site can ask users to review a business or even incentivize people to post reviews. Search engines place more weight on these reviews because your business or brand is not part of the equation.

Then there are reviews that your business or brand solicits or incentivizes. These are against the terms of service of sites like Google, Amazon, or Yelp, but there are plenty of other ways and places you can use them, including your own website. And what's one of the features the search engines look for when indexing your site? Customer reviews!

This is especially true of ecommerce sites. If you sell products on your website, your product pages need customer reviews to deliver a more satisfying visitor experience. Potential shoppers want to see what others think of a product or service before they buy. But search engines can also index and see this content on your product pages, giving them more depth and relevance for related keywords.

The right way to solicit reviews is to do so only when you plan to use them on sites that allow them, including your own. The wrong way is to incentivize customers to post reviews on sites whose terms of service do not allow paid or solicited reviews of a product or service.

Even if you do find a rating or review site that allows solicited or even paid reviews, the FTC requires the reviewer to disclose any paid or benefits-driven relationship behind the review. Even if you just gave the person free product to test, they must state that clearly in the review.

HOW TO USE INFLUENCE MARKETING FOR REVIEWS

Now that we have a clear understanding of the right and wrong way to handle reviews, let's focus on how to incorporate reviews as part of your influence marketing efforts. Your website is a perfect place to post solicited and even paid reviews.

You must still fully disclose the relationship, but if a sporting goods brand has a review from Brazilian model and soccer influence partner

Raquel Benetti (@raquelfrestyle) featured on its review page, its visitors are apt to be impressed. Even if they don't immediately know who Benetti is, you can emphasize her credibility by displaying her stats: 1.7 million YouTube subscribers and almost 500,000 Facebook followers.

Now think about scaling your site reviews to include dozens of influence partners or micro-influence participants. If your site offers ecommerce, imagine having a credible, recognized influence review on every product page. If customers are praising your products alongside influential customers or partners, your product pages will have more impact because they mix customer reviews with expert reviews, the two most important purchase recommendation indicators you can impact.

Then there's the influence partner's website and channels. Search engines don't just look at reviews—they also look at inbound links. If your influence partners have blogs or websites in addition to their social channels, asking them to post a review there can provide your website with an important inbound link as well as a review on a website that is a trusted resource for their audience.

In this way, you are optimizing for search algorithms that lead searchers to your site but also drawing in target customers who may just be going to their favorite influential person's website for regular tips, tricks, or entertaining content. A review there is less ratings-and-review content and more personal endorsement content—even better!

Five Simple Steps to Optimize Your Website for Search Engines

In online marketing, search engine optimization (SEO) may be the most important marketing tactic of all. Ranking high for keywords or keyword phrases people search for on Google, Bing, Yahoo!, or any number of other search engines means more than just drawing traffic to your website. Searchers are low-hanging fruit. If they find your site via a search, they're already looking for what you sell.

Five Simple Steps, continued

There are hundreds of books, blogs, videos, and seminars out there to help you understand SEO better. But here are five simple things you can do regularly to make sure your website is working for you instead of just sitting there:

1. *Publish content regularly.* One of the big factors in search algorithms is recency. If the content on your website is stale, the search engines care about it less. Blogs, articles, new images, videos, or even simple price updates will give search spiders something to read and report back as new.

2. *Write for searchers.* A headline that says, "You'll love the aroma with this in your bathroom" might please a human being visiting your site (assuming there's an appealing picture of a lavender candle under it). But you will rank better for searches with a headline like "Great-smelling lavender candle to get rid of bathroom smells." Why? Because people search for phrases like "lavender candle" and "get rid of bathroom smells." They don't search for "you'll love this aroma" or "this in your bathroom."

3. *Make it mobile.* If your website looks very small on a cell phone, it isn't optimized for mobile. Stop what you're doing and invest in a new design or template that is mobile-friendly. More than 50 percent of searches on Google now come from mobile devices. It makes no sense for them to send that traffic to you if your site doesn't function well for a mobile user, so they won't. Not to mention, a poor mobile experience will turn off any actual visitors.

4. *Use video.* Not only does video make your website more dynamic and personal, but that extra "oomph" of content also adds titles and descriptions that give you more chances to optimize the page for certain keywords.

> ## Five Simple Steps, continued
>
> Oh, and then the video can rank in search results by itself, too, so there's another opportunity to capture more visitors.
>
> 5. *Claim your business.* Google My Business, and similar business listings on Bing and other search engines, are critical to your business's SEO. Set up your profile; put in your name, address, phone number, and business hours; and upload some pictures. This is where you'll send people to review your business, and it's an important factor the search engines consider when evaluating your business and its website.

There are also ratings and review sites that do accept solicited and even paid reviews. They are typically found in niche industries and may not carry the same weight or cachet as those that don't and are thus assumed to be more honest. But they are there. Search for reviews of your business or look at the inbound traffic sources on your website's analytics to find potential review sites. Then look at their terms of service to see if it's OK to direct people there to post reviews.

A REVIEW FOR A LUXURIOUS NIGHT'S SLEEP

Online reviews were a piece of a larger influence program my colleagues at Cornett built for the luxury mattress company Stearns & Foster. Their handcrafted mattresses are a high-end product, so getting that expert, third-party opinion is critically important in an era when cheap, mail order mattresses in a box are trending.

Fortunately, the brand team at Stearns & Foster knows the value of their product and the value of influence partner's content. They reached out to 40 social media influence prospects in the interior design space with the offer of a free luxury mattress in exchange for some content. That content included Instagram and Facebook posts but also an honest review of the mattress to be posted on the company's website.

Six of the 40 went above the contracted ask by posting additional content via Instagram Stories or blog posts.

The goal of the campaign was to generate a million online impressions. It garnered almost double that, thanks to 75 separate posts resulting in almost 150,000 comments, reactions, and shares. But those all-important reviews were part of the payoff, too.

Visitors to stearnsandfoster.com now see reviews from influential interior design creators saying things like, "To have our new mattress from Stearns & Foster has been a life-changing experience." And "My husband and I absolutely love this mattress! It is so important to have great sleep, and this mattress surely does the trick!"

In this example, the online reviews were a secondary ask of the influence partners, beyond the primary Instagram and Facebook campaign. But they can be the main reason you choose to engage influence partners in the first place. What better payoff for you than to have a potential customer click onto your site's review page, only to find one from an influential creator they follow?

But you should consider adding online reviews to any influence program you manage. Even if it is overshadowed by the influence partner's content on Instagram, YouTube, or Facebook, the payoff is multiplied from a search engine standpoint. The inbound links from the influence partner's blogs or websites are giving you added SEO value. The traffic from their social channels is also sending positive signals to the search engines on your behalf. And when the visitors get to your site, they see a credible voice recommending the product in your reviews.

LEVERAGING SOCIAL CONTENT AS ONLINE REVIEWS

What if I told you that all those Instagram and Facebook posts from your chosen influence partners could be repurposed as your website's reviews? And that you could measure and track each one for revenue and effectiveness?

Dropps (dropps.com), a mail order laundry pod company, does this exceptionally well. While I don't think they originally intended to use social posts as their online reviews, it works seamlessly. Using a third-party software plug-in called Curalate (curalate.com), Dropps presents its influence posts in photo galleries on its website. Each post is tagged with the products shown, so the visitor sees social proof (a type of review, if you will) of the product used in context. Curalate's technology allows the user to then click on the post and be presented with an "add-to-cart" opportunity.

Dropps is purpose-led. Their focus on sustainable practices, like no animal testing and plant-based ingredients, is a compelling narrative to social-savvy younger adults. It had the functional mechanism it needed to turn social content into cart-filling visual reviews on its website. Now it needed a bunch of influence partner content featuring the product to fill those slots.

The brand turned to ApexDrop, a specialty influence agency that scales and sends product gifts to micro-influence prospects. They sourced 700 different influence partners and more than 800 social posts Dropps could present on its website as visual and contextual "reviews." The cost? Just free product sent to the influence partners and the fees ApexDrop charged to manage the campaign.

These "Fan Reels," as they call the social-media-as-reviews posts, increased visitor time on the site by more than 200 percent and conversion rates by 174 percent. Dropps' average order value for Fan Reel visitors, as compared to those who don't shop them, is even higher.

THE POWER OF PRODUCT-ONLY PAYMENT

ABBY&FINN (abbyandfinn.com) is another brand that uses the Fan Reel approach, where influence partners' social posts can serve as image-driven, contextual reviews on the brand website. The subscription service offers diapers and wipes shipped direct to your door in your choice of frequency, sizes, and designs. You can even choose mixed-size boxes for those unanticipated growth spurts.

ABBY&FINN also uses Curalate and sources influence content through ApexDrop, which exclusively uses the product-for-post approach. They don't offer influence partners cash payments.

"There's a fine line between paying someone to post about you, then a month later they're posting about another brand because they're getting paid," said Amanda Little, ABBY&FINN's cofounder. "We really wanted to focus on growing organically and partner with people who are in-line with our mission."

That mission includes addressing the fact that one in three U.S. families face challenges even getting diapers. So for every subscription box they sell, they donate 30 diapers to a charity that provides them to needy families.

"We don't have huge marketing budgets, but we are able to pay influencers in product," Little explained. "By not just writing them a check, they can then speak more genuinely about their experience."

She said an influence partner's audience then trusts their perception of ABBY&FINN more. Why would the creator accept a free product and post about it if they didn't like it? Of course, there's always a chance the person could post a critical or negative review, but that's fine by the brand.

"Aside from a couple of tags we ask them to use, we don't give them a lot of guidance," Little said. "That works best because they know their followers best. If they were to post something that was scripted and not authentic, their followers would spot it. That reflects poorly on them and on the brand. We leave it as open-ended as possible."

That approach only requires brands to possess one thing: Confidence that they have a great product.

BE INTENTIONAL ABOUT REVIEWS

The possibilities associated with leveraging influence partners for online reviews are there for the taking. Tools like Curalate can elevate a reviews page into an image-driven, add-to-cart weapon for your website. But you'll need great content to populate its carousels, and that's where influence partners come in.

Other review tools like Trustpilot (trustpilot.com) allow you to point anyone to their platform to post a review about your products or services. You can then pull your reviews from the platform and post them on your site. Why not ask your influence partners to post a review on these platforms as part of their engagement? (With appropriate disclosures, of course.)

As long as you're making sure people you are paying or gifting product to are not posting reviews on sites that forbid it, like Google, Amazon, Yelp, and others, your brand can ask your influence partners for reviews. And it can use them in very powerful ways to attract both search engines and consumers.

If you intentionally plan to leverage reviews from your online influence partners to populate your website, your social channels, and your influence partners' channels, they may also accomplish another of your influence marketing missions: driving word of mouth.

EMPLOYING WORD-OF-MOUTH INFLUENCE (ENTHUSE)

"Word-of-mouth marketing is 62 times more effective than advertising." That sentence was drilled into me when I worked at Doe-Anderson, the Louisville ad agency that helped create the Maker's Mark Ambassadors Club, one of the gold standards in word-of-mouth marketing.

I don't recall where they got that number, but it doesn't matter. It's an old statistic and was probably misinterpreted through several chains of people before it got to me, but it still resonates. Strong word-of-mouth marketing, or "WOMM" (rhymes with mom), as those in the industry call it, is the calling card of some of my favorite brands.

The aforementioned Maker's Mark Ambassadors program allows those who sign up to have their name etched on a gold plate on a single barrel of bourbon. The brand then sends you updates about your barrel throughout its aging process (which lasts five to seven years). When the barrel is ready, it then invites you to the distillery in Loretto, Kentucky, to claim your personalized bottles of bourbon, with your name printed on the label.

Ambassadors feel like they own the brand. Why wouldn't they? Their name is on a barrel! And what do you think they do with that sense of pride? They tell their friends. Who then also become Ambassadors. And so on.

While one could argue that any compelling marketing campaign could be given credit for driving word of mouth, also sometimes referred to as "buzz," there's a difference between someone mentioning a clever TV ad and intentionally talking to their friends about a product.

This chapter will explain what word-of-mouth programs really are. You'll hear from expert practitioners on how influential people fit into a word-of-mouth strategy. And I'll show you three more case studies that deliver on WOMM from a Winfluence perspective.

TRUE WORD-OF-MOUTH IS A STRATEGY

Just like advertising is a strategy to reach masses of people with a message quickly, and repeating the message reinforces it to change perceptions or behavior, word-of-mouth marketing is a strategy. Pure word-of-mouth marketing bakes your brand into people's minds so they naturally talk about you, whether they're prompted to or not.

The key that makes it "pure" word-of-mouth marketing is that they talk about you organically. As a divorced dad who struggles to cook anything, much less healthy meals for me and my children, I often sing the praises of EveryPlate. The subscription service sends all the meat, veggies, and other ingredients I need to cook three meals a week, along with easy-to-follow recipe cards, right to my door. I've even set it to deliver on Wednesdays, the day I get my son and daughter from their mother each week.

On Wednesday, Thursday, and every other Friday night, I can cook well-portioned, fresh, healthy meals without needing to plan or even go to the grocery store to buy ingredients. The three meals (which actually become four since each recipe makes enough for four people) cost me less per week than a typical night out at a casual dining restaurant.

Those two paragraphs above are pure word-of-mouth marketing. EveryPlate isn't a client. Other than being a customer, I've had no official communication with the company. (I sure would like to, though, and am cleverly including them in my book.)

I'm a fan and advocate of EveryPlate because for me, their service goes far beyond what it promises to. I'm no longer a deficient dad in the meals department. My children are eating healthier and trying new foods. And my daughter cooks with me, so EveryPlate has given me a stronger connection with her.

Word-of-mouth marketing looks to identify customers and community members who will have that reaction to a brand and spread the good word. It might be that you're looking for people like me, who are overserved in value by the product, so you can learn their stories. Or you might want to connect with existing customers you can tell those stories to, so they become more passionate about the brand.

"I think that word-of-mouth marketing is a discipline," Ted Wright told me. He's the CEO of Fizz, a pioneering word-of-mouth marketing agency that lists legendary WOMM programs like Pabst Blue Ribbon (which they took from almost dead to first in its category) among its many case studies. "WOMM requires you to focus on conversation and creating an opportunity for one consumer to have a conversation with another."

Most word-of-mouth marketing case studies don't focus on online influencers but rather empowered consumers. Still, an influential person armed with the information, resources, and inspiration to talk about your brand and spark conversations—and who happens to have lots of social media followers—is a bonus.

"Word of mouth is irrespective of where you're having the conversation," Wright explained. "We are agnostic about the tool, but we are fundamentalists in our belief that the most effective marketing is driven by conversations between two people who know one another."

Wright said conversations can start online, off-line, or even simultaneously in both places. He mentioned, however, that online is appealing to marketers because it's easier to measure. When conversations happen on digital platforms, where views, retweets, comments, and more are recorded and measured, you can see that one person caused a dozen more to pass the word. But online is not where word-of-mouth marketing is won or lost, because that's not where most conversations happen.

"At this point, we know 70 percent of word-of-mouth conversations happen off-line," Wright said, citing his company's extensive research. "And that's face-to-face. Seventy percent are face-to-face, 20 percent are over the phone, and only 10 percent of them are in the world of social media."

"Online influencers can be fire starters for your brand. There's a role for them," argued Geno Church, a Word of Mouth Marketing Association hall of famer. "The challenge is that a lot of brands put their money in one bucket and don't look at different types of influential people holistically."

Church said true fire starters are the "1 percenters" who will literally take you to a ballgame or a favorite restaurant or bring you an album they think you should listen to. "That's the holy grail," he said. "Right beneath them is an advocate. Nine out of ten brands have advocates but don't give them a job to do. They might follow you and like your content online, but what can we do to get them to participate?"

Word-of-mouth programs, then, create opportunities for existing advocates to learn more about a brand and share it, or for casual consumers to become advocates and do the same. Those advocates can be people with influence, but the litmus test of whether it is true advocacy boils down to authenticity.

IS PAYMENT AN AUTHENTICITY KILLER?

Does a paid relationship hurt an influential person's impact on their audience? Not according to current research on the subject. *Harvard Business Review* contributors Alice Audrezet and Karine Charry, both academicians and researchers, polled consumers in 2017, when the FTC issued stronger requirements for online influencers to disclose brand relationships in their content. They took another poll a year later.

The polls gauged people's overall opinion of a brand and their judgment of its trustworthiness after its relationship with an online influencer was disclosed. They also measured whether the disclosure affected consumers' purchase intention. Consumers viewed a brand slightly more negatively in 2017 after disclosure, but a year later that difference had disappeared. In the other two areas measured, there was no statistical difference in consumers' attitudes toward brands that disclosed relationships with influence partners and brands that did not.

The disclosure factor may even reinforce the importance of influential voices as a resource for purchasing decisions. In the 2018 poll, 88 percent of consumers said they believe the reason influential people recommend brands is because the companies are paying them to do so. So even when a post recommending a brand doesn't contain a disclosure, the influential person's audience probably assumes they're getting paid anyway.

Audrezet and Charry wrote in the *HBR* article: "In this context, disclosure becomes a positive signal: savvy consumers value the perceived transparency and authenticity of influencers who volunteer a disclose."

Kristy Sammis, executive director of the Influencer Marketing Association, also disagrees with the sponsored-is-bad argument. "People want to be sponsored," she said. "It's a legitimizing force.

"The data suggests it is not the case," she added. "We are all so media savvy, even our kids are, that we understand advertisements are everywhere. We are being sold to all the time. The more upfront you are about it, people are like, 'Oh. OK.'"

Sammis also pointed out that "the kids" are now calling it "collabs." Ask anyone born after 2000 what they think of an influential person they follow doing a collab with a brand, and they'll be happy for that person. That at least offers anecdotal validation that brand sponsorships for influence partners are badges of honor, not a source of skepticism.

Church didn't argue with the numbers, but he does think that building word of mouth is a long-term play, and an influence campaign isn't going to be as effective.

"Paying an influencer runs its course. It's like a campaign that lasts 30, 60, or 90 days," he explained. "You still need to figure out your sustainability. That's the power of word of mouth—the sustainability."

While the data suggests their audiences don't distinguish between paid and unpaid (or at least undisclosed) influence posts, the holy grail of word-of-mouth marketing comes after the payments stop and there's no extrinsic benefit. That's when the subjects of your influence efforts are still recommending you to people.

"Are you renting someone's time or are you renting someone's mind?" Wright asked. "If you're renting someone's time, that's legit."

In other words, if you have to pay them to say or think good things about you, and those words and thoughts stop when their payment or extrinsic benefit ends, that's not word of mouth. If you pay them for the time they invest in officially producing content or work for you, but they continue to share their love of you even after "renting their time" ends, you have WOMM success.

Wright said there are two kinds of online influencers in a word-of-mouth scenario. The first is someone a brand pays to do something they would already do—they just do it more. He calls these people advocates. The second is someone who takes your money to broadcast your message, whether they would have recommended it before or not.

Wright's team at Fizz labels this second type *broadcasters* rather than influencers. Like TV networks, they just put your ad up for people to see. When I asked him if he thought many broadcasters had enough integrity to only recommend brands they genuinely liked, he laughed.

"With all the brands we've worked with in 20-plus years, I've only seen 'influencers' walk away from two paychecks," he said. "I'm sure that everybody says, 'I have integrity.' But when push comes to shove, everyone takes the money."

INFLUENCE PARTNERS ARE WORD-OF-MOUTH FIRE STARTERS

So let's be honest: A lot of what you see on online influencers' accounts, especially in this era of influence marketing agencies, software services, and huge social networks, is straight pay-for-placement. They're ads. And many influential people online are charging for what they can provide in audience exposure.

But I've been building influence relationships for more than 25 years. I know large projects that consume their time, or rely on them to create engaging content on the client's behalf, almost always require remuneration. I also have several influential people working with clients who are simply their partners. They watch the client's feed and engage with its posts. They voluntarily provide social shares and feedback and are happy to hop on a call to brainstorm ideas for the brand.

As Wright explained, it's a question of whether you are renting their time or their mind. Influential people who are leasing us their time but believe in the product eventually become true advocates for the brand. They get paid, but it's so they can have more time and opportunity to work for something they really care about. At that point, the paid influence relationship evolves into the word-of-mouth holy grail.

Remember the University of Kentucky HealthCare film influence program we discussed in Chapter 7? My team at Cornett worked with UK HealthCare to produce an inspirational video highlighting its care practices and caregivers. We identified 43 local and regional social media influence partners, but we also had a long list of people with off-line influence we wanted to engage with the video and share it with their networks.

A year later, UK HealthCare produced a "Thank You" video to express their appreciation to everyone during the COVID-19 outbreak. The quick-cut snippets from various influential people thanked everyone from front-line health-care workers and grocery clerks stocking shelves to food delivery drivers and people electing to stay home and prevent the spread of the virus. The same partners were asked to participate. They all volunteered.

Church has three categories of influential people in word-of-mouth marketing: influencer, advocate, and evangelist. An influencer might help inform people about your product, service, or even community. An advocate truly believes in what you do and would talk about you if prompted. An evangelist passionately creates content and helps you every chance they get because they have some deep intrinsic connection to your brand; they wear you like a badge of honor.

UK HealthCare's "We Are Proof" campaign started with influential people, on- and off-line. Thanks to their previous experiences with the brand and the creativity of the film, most of them became advocates. By the time the opportunity to contribute to the COVID-19 "Thank You" project came along, all of them were advocates. Several were evangelists.

Using influential people to ignite your word-of-mouth efforts is like buying self-pollinating plants at Lowe's. You bring them home, plant them, and in a year or two, you have a dozen or more plants that can produce a dozen more and so on. The difference is that in word-of-mouth marketing, you typically don't want to control the growth.

GOT (CHOCOLATE) MILK?

Wright's agency, Fizz, produced one of the best examples of off-line influence marketing I've seen to date. The American Dairy Association hired them to help reverse their falling milk sales. One of their goals was to get preteens and teenagers to keep drinking milk beyond elementary school, when they typically slowed consumption.

Armed with research that showed chocolate milk was one of the best things to drink after a workout, Fizz targeted football coaches across the test state of Ohio with mailers and other information, so they would encourage their athletes to drink more. They engaged former NFL and Major League Baseball players and state championship athletes to show up at football clinics and help spread the word about the power of drinking chocolate milk.

The new "trend" was even picked up and reported on by ESPN.

In the focus state of Ohio, milk consumption jumped 16 percent in one year. Over a four-year span that included Fizz's campaign, the Ohio milk industry saw sales increase 475 percent.

Fizz even says on its website, "High school football coaches across our test state of Ohio were our influencers." Yet the campaign had nothing to do with Instagram, Facebook, or TikTok.

Looking at this campaign through the Winfluence filter, it clearly follows the model that word of mouth comes through influence, not influencers. There was no online component. This campaign worked through the off-line influence of football coaches.

To boot, every bit of the strategy ladders up to the overall business goal of increasing consumption. While Wright and others would call this WOMM and not specifically influence marketing, they identified people of influence and used them to persuade an audience to change their behavior to accomplish a strategic purpose. That's Winfluence.

CREATING WORD OF MOUTH ACROSS A BRAND PORTFOLIO

Large consumer product goods companies, like Procter & Gamble, Unilever, Nestlé, and Kellogg's, often have dozens of brands and even more influence marketing programs at play at any given time. Most of the time, a single brand's efforts happen within the silo of that brand. But Kraft Canada came up with a neat word-of-mouth extension of influence marketing for its portfolio of food and snack products.

In 2010–2011 and then again in 2014, Kraft managed a sampling program aimed at influential content creators to spark recommendations and awareness of brands like Crystal Light, Jell-O, and Kraft Mayo. Mom bloggers and other online influence partners were targeted based on something the brand called "talkability" factor—a measure of how frequently they talked about and recommended products.

Each sampler packet wasn't given to the influence targets but sold to them. That's right . . . the targeted creators paid for the packets. Granted, each contained roughly $40 to $50 worth of items and they sold for less than $15, and the prospects Kraft targeted were certainly in the vertical of coupon-clippers and efficient homemaking content. But if paying influential people can diminish the effectiveness of their recommendations, then if they pay for the product and recommend it, that should magnify it, right?

The original program sold 15,000 sample packets to influence participants over four days. That led to more than a quarter of a million product trials. Sales lifts for the products included in the samplers ranged from 30 percent to 325 percent over two months.

Is this a Winfluence campaign? Certainly. The goal was to drive trial of a variety of products through online influencers they knew would post about the samples. Increased reach and frequency of the brands mentioned meant increased awareness and at least the potential of an increase in sales.

The influence partners were chosen for their online presence and because their audiences were apt to follow advice from coupon-clipping homemaker types. The focus was on the influence, not just on picking influencers.

That's Winfluence.

THE MAGIC OF MUTUALLY BENEFICIAL ORGANIC INFLUENCE

Meredith Noble's grant writing courses can turn just about anyone into a successful grant writer. She's so good at teaching the skill that she started LearnGrantWriting.org to offer both free and paid courses to share her expertise.

While she would certainly love to have dozens of government and nonprofit experts telling the world to go take her courses, she approached influence marketing in a more organic way that turned out to be mutually beneficial.

Noble encourages her audience to use Instrumentl (instrumentl. com), a subscription-based grant database for nonprofits. She doesn't have any personal ties to the company, but she offers affiliate links to sign up to Instrumentl in her content. She does get a commission for each new subscriber she sends their way, so in a sense Noble is an influence partner for the service.

However, that activity opened an avenue for Instrumentl to influence people on Noble's behalf. When she published her 2019 book *How to Write a Grant: Become a Grant Writing Unicorn*, Noble asked Instrumentl

CEO Gauri Manglik to read the manuscript. If she liked it and would be willing to provide one, Noble would use a testimonial quote from her on the book's back cover. Manglik did, and her quote gave the book and Noble's online courses more credibility.

Then, a few months later, a student in Noble's program forwarded an email she had received from Instrumentl. It was a response to a lead inquiry from a company representative. The postscript of the email said, "If you're just getting started, we recommend this book as a resource: *How to Write a Grant: Becoming a Grant Writing Unicorn.*"

An affiliate marketer, which is a type of influence partner, sends leads to a company. They then ask for an endorsement for a book. Then they organically get leads back from recommendations from the company! While many would say the affiliate nature of Noble's initial relationship with Instrumentl is more akin to advertising, the mutual recommendations certainly fall into the category of influencing someone to try or consider a service.

But the attention Noble generated with her mentions, affiliate leads, and book quote request led to an organic, natural, word-of-mouth endorsement from the company to its prospects. That's just a neatly wrapped package of awesome.

The key takeaway from Noble's example is to know that influence marketing doesn't have to be an intricately planned campaign. It can also be the result of influencing on your part or building a relationship without a formal quid pro quo payoff in mind. Strategically targeting and promoting influence prospects (or partners) who may reap rewards from your audience is a very smart way to begin a relationship where they can ultimately promote you.

WORD OF MOUTH IS THE HOLY GRAIL OF INFLUENCE MARKETING

Word-of-mouth marketing, it can be argued, is the ultimate in influence marketing. It leverages people of influence and arms them with the tools, knowledge, or resources they need to genuinely refer and recommend your brand to others. The best examples are a magic confluence of persuasion (*My team should drink more milk*), association (*Users of this grant software should read this book . . . and readers of the book should use this grant software*), validation (*EveryPlate makes even my sorry ass a good cook!*), and enthusiasm (*I'm bragging to my friends that my name is on a barrel of Maker's Mark!*).

Every influence marketing strategy ever created would have paid off exponentially if the initial lift the brand manufactured through people of influence had led to them and their followers becoming advocates for the brand. Word-of-mouth marketing doesn't have to be the official mission of your influence marketing programs. But at the end of the day, becoming the subject of an incredible word-of-mouth marketing case study is what you're shooting for.

Now that we have an ultimate target, let's spend some time examining how we know if or when we've hit it and take a look at measuring influence marketing.

— chapter —

15

MEASURING INFLUENCE SUCCESS

Barbara Jones has been a part of influence market-ing since the formative days of blog conferences. She was the founder of influence marketing agency Blissful Media Group and created Blissdom, one of the early events that brought influential online personalities together with brands. She now manages top TikTok creators at Outshine Talent. Jones says the industry hasn't changed that much when you look at the measurement piece of the puzzle.

"Still, to this day, there aren't benchmarks," she said. "There aren't pricing structures. There are 101 ways to measure metrics, and nobody can agree on which ones make the most sense. It's more than ten years later, and it's still the Wild West."

For her part, Jones has been instrumental in organizing the Influencer Marketing Association (IMA), one of the first attempts at a professional organization that aims to protect the authenticity and ethics of influence marketing.

"We want to pull people together who want to make this work," she said. "If we don't and we don't legitimize the industry, we're one Fyre Festival away from collapsing."

At this writing, the IMA is still in the planning stages for establishing suggested rules and regulations for ethical standards addressing working in the industry. It hopes to streamline expectations and benchmarks around metrics, standards, and practices. (Full disclosure: I am a paying member of IMA, but it remains to be seen how effective the organization can be.)

To have the industry follow the rules, guidelines, and ethical standards of an organization, the entire industry has to buy into the organization. And the one thing we know about those who have built influence via social media is that they don't respect traditional approaches or constraints.

This chapter is where we cut through the confusion and get down to brass tacks. In it, you'll learn how to measure and focus on your goals. You'll see the ins and outs of planning to measure and how that pays off in the end. We'll wrap it up with a handy Winfluence Success Scorecard you can put to use with your next campaign.

WE CAN'T WAIT ON AGREEMENT

Brands and their marketers have two choices: wait on the industry to tell us how to measure or figure it out for ourselves. Most agencies and brands have chosen the latter, but not without a lot of grumbling.

Ask most marketers what their top challenge is with any of their influence marketing programs, and inevitably measuring success is high on the list. In a 2018 study by Linqia, the biggest challenge with influence marketing for marketers was determining campaign ROI.

Measurement struggles across all marketing channels have always baffled me, to be honest. ROI is an accounting measure that determines what percentage of your spend you got back in revenue. You can't measure a financial return if you aren't trying to drive financial transactions. If you want to measure ROI on a campaign, then your goal has to be to drive sales. If your goal is something else, you cannot measure ROI.

The most common problem I see in marketing managers who say they have trouble determining ROI is that their goals are not focused on revenue. Measuring ROI then becomes frustrating, as they can't even get the proper numbers for their equation. They're asking the wrong question.

Still, the most common measure of success with influence marketing campaigns today is sales or conversions. According to the Influencer Marketing Hub's "The State of Influencer Marketing 2020: Benchmark Report," 39 percent of marketers tie the success of an influence marketing campaign to the number of sales or conversions it brings in. Thirty-four percent measure success through engagement or clicks, and 27 percent do so with views, reach, and impressions.

ROI should be part of the conversation. But if it's not part of your goals, then asking about the ROI is the wrong question.

MEASUREMENT IS ALL ABOUT GOALS

How do you know whether you've succeeded in doing something? You compare the outcome to your original intent. You can always claim to be successful, but if you cannot outline the specific details of what you set out to do compared to where you wound up, your success is vague and unconvincing. Unless you have a CEO or board of directors that doesn't care much about details, you cannot report success with ambiguity.

Why, then, would anyone attempt to measure success without first tying that success to the campaign or program's original intention?

At the campaign level, everything should revolve around your goal. I've often argued with clients that we are more likely to succeed if we zero in on just one goal. That keeps our focus from being cloudy. Perhaps your goal is to increase sales, but you also want to improve customer service. If that's the case, separate them into two campaigns. If you don't, you'll confuse everyone, and your campaign won't do as well.

Let's say you choose the goal of increasing sales. Under that goal, you will have objectives, often thought of in measurement terms as key performance indicators, or KPIs. These might include increasing brand awareness, website traffic, online reviews, online influence referrals, and so on. But they are all building blocks that fit together to make the ultimate goal: sell more stuff.

Your goal is not a KPI. It is not a *key* performance indicator. It is THE performance indicator. You either did it or you didn't. Everything else explains why.

To measure your influence campaigns, then, you have to work hard on the front end to clearly define your goal and outline the various objectives you will activate (and measure) to understand on the back end whether you succeeded.

THE IMPERATIVE OF GOAL CLARITY

Clearly defining your influence marketing goals from the outset is the most important step you can take to properly measuring success. Remember my analogy in Chapter 5 about waiting to measure success until the end of the campaign? It's like waiting until you get to the end of the driveway with your family to ask, "OK, where are we going on vacation?"

Without a destination in mind, you'll never know if you arrive. You need to know your goal from the beginning. Also in Chapter 5, we talked about what influence marketing can do for your business. The five business drivers were these:

1. Influential people can drive brand awareness.
2. Influential people can help protect your reputation.
3. Influential people can help build your audience or community.
4. Influential people can supplement R&D.
5. Influential people can drive direct leads or sales.

The more clearly defined your goal is, the more effectively you can design measurement systems to validate how much or how far you get in achieving it. If your goal is to drive brand awareness, measure how many people are aware of your brand at the beginning of, or before, the campaign starts. Then you measure the same thing after your campaign has run for a given period of time and compare the two.

To be even clearer, say your goal is to increase brand awareness among mothers of teens in Milwaukee by 25 percent in 12 months. Developing a measurement system for that goal is very easy. Survey the mothers of teens in Milwaukee before the campaign starts to check their awareness of your product. Survey the mothers of teens in Milwaukee 12 months later and ask the same questions. The difference in their answers is your level of success.

You might think that marketing campaigns are often layered and complex, so measurement can't be that simple. My argument is that it not only can be, but it should be. All those other things you're measuring are KPIs to help you adjust your approach and make sure you meet THE performance indicator. Sometimes they're just performance indicators, and they're not key to anything. Then you can safely ignore them.

So let's define our goal so we can get rid of the PIs—and even some of the KPIs—and focus on measuring THE PI.

MEASUREMENT MAPPING

You have your goal. Regardless of how complex or simple it is, you now need to plan to measure. The plan comes together by mapping out the what, when, how, where, and who of your measurement program.

If your goal is increasing sales, you will need to collect retail or sales data, but you also must be able to separate and attribute that data to your influence campaign. Are you sending all the influence partner's traffic to a specific landing page so you can isolate it? Are you asking them to share unique coupon codes? Do you have a mechanism in your ecommerce or retail system to track the number of coupon codes used?

If increasing followers is the goal of your influence marketing campaign, you may need to tap into social network APIs to pull in data for analysis. You may need to access a measurement software solution to unify all your social network information together and make this task fluid and consistent.

A good tactical goal for an influence marketing campaign might be to increase your email subscribers. Do you have a tagging system set up in your email service software to segment new subscribers from the influence partner's channels, or are you giving the partner special links or forms to use for their audiences?

We spent much of the previous chapter talking about driving word-of-mouth marketing, which often manifests in online buzz. Do you have a social listening platform deployed to measure what your buzz is now before you start your campaign?

Those are all examples of mapping the "how" behind *your* analytics, which is just the beginning of your measurement mapping. You also need to collect and analyze the data from your influence partners.

Let's say you have influence partners posting on Facebook or Instagram as part of your program. You also have them using the popular Stories feature on both platforms. You won't be able to tell how many likes their Instagram posts get, since the network hid like counts in early 2020.

So you'll need to plan to measure your influence partners, too. Ask about that upfront when negotiating with them. You will need to find out:

* Will they send you their success metrics in an email? A spreadsheet?
* If you use an influence marketing platform, will they allow it to pull their analytics automatically and share them with you?
* When will they do this?
* How often will they report back to you?
* If they are self-reporting, will you require screenshots for validation, or do you trust them to report honestly?

How sophisticated your data collection and analysis can be depends primarily on your resources. At larger organizations, you can work with your data or analytics teams to build dashboards and automatically import the data you need to see.

Smaller organizations may need to find an analytics platform or combination of platforms that can help you. Google Analytics is free and can give you numbers from your website ranging from how many users visited to which pages they navigated to, to what country they are visiting from and what links they click on while there. Some social media management software can create reports showing everything from your own channels as well as from online mentions through monitoring software.

A small business should, at minimum, pull the most relevant metrics into a spreadsheet that can be updated frequently and shared among the stakeholders.

In Figure 15–1 below you can see an example of a measurement map I created for a fictional B2B company called Acme Equipment. It lays out the measurement plan for a lead-generation campaign driven by downloads of an annual industry report on the company's website.

The goal of the campaign is to drive leads through the report download, and in the map, I've listed out eight primary sources of traffic where those leads will come from. Down the left side of the map, I have the sources from Acme Equipment: website article, website banner, email promotions, and social media posts. All those are on Acme's website and social media channels or from Acme's email marketing.

On the right side of the map, I have listed outside sources of traffic (that is, ones not owned by Acme) used in the campaign: online media, retargeting, pay-per-click ads, and influencer partners. I even listed out my

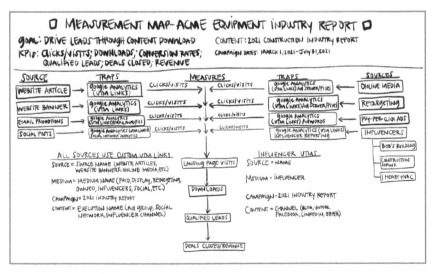

figure 15–1. A Measurement Map Example

three partners: Bob's Building, Construction Hawk, and I Heart HVAC (all invented for this exercise).

The traffic from each source travels through traps, where I will measure certain activity so that I can report and analyze the success of the campaign. Every source will be assigned UTM-coded links so I can use Google Analytics as my primary reporting platform.

By using different UTM links for each of the eight sources, I can drill down to a Google Analytics report by campaign and see all eight sources in one report. You'll notice in the lower-left corner of the map I have a list of the UTM parameters used in the campaign. The one that is always the same is "Campaign," for this very reason.

On the lower right, I have a list of the influence partner UTM parameters. The source parameter will be the name of the partner. So "Bob's Building" will be the source in the links I assign to him, "Construction Hawk" will be the source in the one I give to that partner, and so on.

The medium for influence partners is "Influence" so I can filter my reports in Google Analytics and just show the metrics for my influence program for this campaign. As I explained earlier, the Campaign doesn't change. But the Content parameter allows me to give each influence partner a different link to use on each of their channels. That way I can see in Google Analytics how many leads came from I Heart HVAC's blog vs. their YouTube channel, their Facebook page, and so on.

I've also used the Content parameter to separate out ads focused on different audience segments. So if I don't care which channel my partners' leads are coming from, I can instead assign a parameter called "HVAC" for all my partners who appeal to a heating and cooling audience and another one called "Construction" for those with that primary audience. This allows me to see which target consumer converts better through that particular source.

The additional traps, like the Ad Server/Pixel for Online Media and Retargeting, remind me that I can also analyze data from my online media or retargeting software or service to doublecheck my Google Analytics data. They also remind me I will need to install a tracking pixel from those services on my website to ensure their reports are aligned.

Planning to measure in this way not only makes the resulting reports more useful but also makes frequent checks and course corrections possible.

DEPLOY THE MECHANISMS

When your mapping is done, you will have a blueprint for measurement success. You know your goal or goals and what metrics will illustrate whether or how much you've succeeded with them. You will have a schedule for check-ins and benchmarking the campaign. And you will know where to get your analytics.

Now you have to launch your campaign and deploy those mechanisms. Turn on your social listening software and set daily alerts to hit your inbox so you can see progress. Check your social and website analytics daily to see what impact the influence efforts are having.

Make sure you have all the software you need, your subscriptions are paid, and the data is either easily accessible or automatically flowing to a dashboard or reporting center where you can monitor it. The more frequently you check, the more quickly you can respond if something is amiss.

I suggest putting a measurement check-in on your calendar every day of the campaign. Even just a 15-minute calendar appointment can remind you and give you time to actually do it. Then put a weekly half-hour or hour calendar item on your schedule to pull together some top-line KPIs or other indicators you can share with the team in an email or spreadsheet.

This frequent monitoring and sharing of success indicators becomes particularly valuable when an influence partner has too little or too much impact on a campaign. If one influence partner is sending so much traffic to your website that the server is crashing, you can react and solve the problem by either increasing server capacity or asking the influence partner to divert their calls to action until you have fixed the problem.

Conversely, if an influence partner doesn't seem to be driving the same type of traffic or engagements you were expecting, or they are falling far short of the other influence channels you are measuring, you can fulfill your commitment to them and move on to someone else.

NOW YOU CAN MEASURE SUCCESS

With a clearly defined goal, a well-constructed map to see the KPIs, and an ultimate number that represents THE PI, you no longer need to fret about understanding what you got out of your influence marketing efforts. Yes, the process of gathering the data may be cumbersome or complex, especially if you can't afford enterprise-level analytics software. But complex isn't hard. It's just time-consuming.

Did you increase ROI through your influence marketing program? Well, you were getting $235 for every $100 spent on marketing before the program. Thanks to your clear goal of driving ROI and a detailed map to collect the information you needed to reflect that work, you can report that for every $100 you spent on influence marketing, you are now earning $312. That is an increased ROI of 67 percent. Your influence marketing program is successful.

In my experience, more than 90 percent of the frustration around measurement comes from not having clearly defined goals and not deploying a plan to measure those goals from the outset. You may have to ask your partners to take screenshots of their Instagram Story metrics, collect those images via email, and manually transcribe the numbers into an Excel document. But if you have a plan, your influence partners cooperate, and you take the time to do the work, measuring your success will be much less painful than others claim it is.

THE WINFLUENCE SUCCESS SCORECARD

The Winfluence Success Scorecard, shown in Figure 15–2 on page 197 and also in Appendix B of this book, is a one-page, quick guide to report the high-level KPIs in your influence programs based on your goals. The primary goals of any influence program broadly fall into five main categories: sales, conversions, traffic, awareness, and perception. I've left a sixth area for "other" in case you have a specific goal besides those five you wish to track.

In this example, I've filled in the Sales Scorecard to illustrate what one would look like for a successful lead-generation B2B campaign for the Acme Equipment Industry Report we used for our measurement map

figure 15–2. The Winfluence Success Scorecard—Sales Example

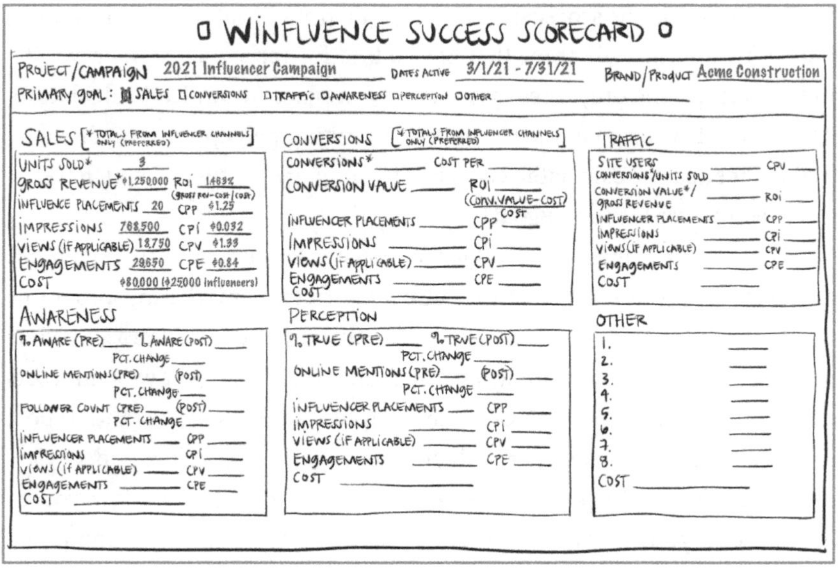

in Figure 15–1. The information here would only be available after the campaign finished, all data from the influence partners was reported, and all subsequent leads and deals were finalized.

You see from the scorecard that we spent $80,000 total on the campaign (Cost) and $25,000 on our influence engagement. We grossed $1,250,000 in revenue from three closed deals—maybe not a huge number, but when your average order value is $400,000-plus, you'll take it, right? Given the $80,000 total cost of the project, that is a 1,463 percent ROI.

We engaged 20 influence partners to talk about and promote the research. We even gave them a short promotional video to use in their content. From our $25,000 influence budget, we earned a cost-per-placement of $1,250 and paid an average of 3 cents per impression, $1.33 per video view, and 84 cents per engagement (which included comments, shares, and likes).

Compared to B2C campaigns, the video view and engagement rates are probably a little high, but again, this is for a B2B company that made an average of $416,667 for each closed deal. I'll take $1.33 per video view and 84 cents per engagement on that all day.

If you look at the scorecard overall, you'll notice that sales, conversions, and traffic are the only three that have a line for reporting monetary KPIs and, therefore, the only ones that also have a place for an ROI calculation. Remember, if your goal is awareness or changing perception, the financial factors needed to calculate ROI aren't going to be there. You have to measure and report to the goal.

The key to using the Winfluence Success Scorecard is to remember it is best deployed over time to compare influence marketing programs and their associated costs. That's why most of the line items in your scorecard have corresponding cost-per entries. You'll know your costs for each program, so you can (and should) always track and report cost per placement, cost per influence impression, cost per video view (if applicable), and cost per engagement. These ratios will allow you to quickly see if your spend on a program was more or less efficient compared with previous efforts.

For sales, conversion, and traffic, note that the metrics of units sold, gross revenue, and conversion value are preferred to come from influence marketing channels only. This is where the "plan to measure" mantra comes in: You'll need to think through how you can separate out units sold, gross revenue, and conversions coming from influence programs. For website conversions and sales, this is easily addressed by the UTM parameters we discussed in Chapter 5. For off-line sales and conversions or those made through point-of-sale or other systems not connected to CRM or website analytics for tracking through UTM, you may need to be more creative. In a worst-case scenario, you can always track the source of a sale by surveying customers after a purchase, asking, "Where did you hear about us?"

In the awareness and perception categories, you'll see pre- and post-campaign measurements because those categories are best explained through the percentage change in awareness, survey answers, or online mentions from the beginning of a campaign to the end. Again, this will require exercising your "plan to measure" muscle. Awareness efforts should always begin with the baseline metric of how many people are currently aware of your company/brand/product. When you measure the same number after a campaign, you can see the change and thus determine the effectiveness of your campaign. The same principle applies to perception answers in surveys. You have to do one beforehand to know how effective the campaign was in changing people's responses. And, of course, the same thing applies to measuring online conversations mentioning a given topic, brand, or talking point. Know how many are happening via a social listening analysis before you can learn how you drive more (or less) conversation around a given point during the campaign.

You can explore more with the Winfluence Success Scorecard at winfluencebook.com.

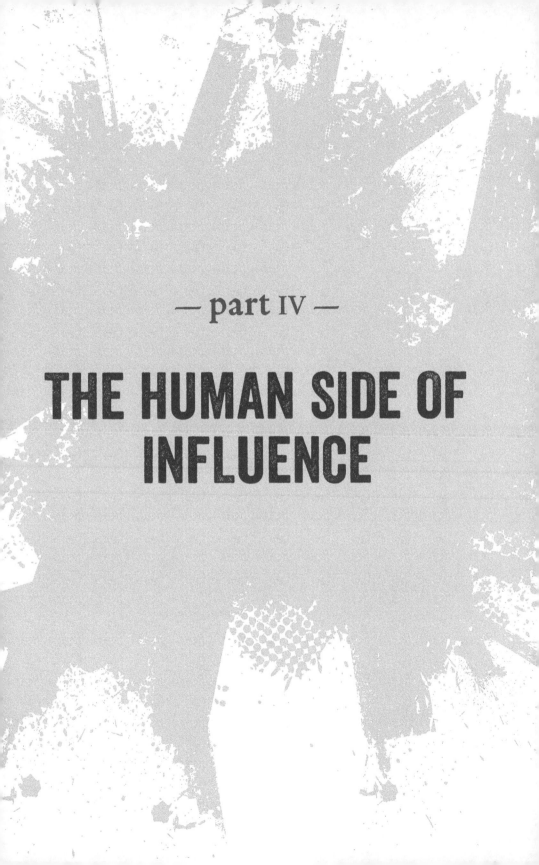

— part IV —

THE HUMAN SIDE OF INFLUENCE

WHERE TECHNOLOGY HURTS, NOT HELPS

Talking about measurement and analytics is fun. Even if you're not a numbers nerd, tracking the data around sales, conversions, engagements, and conversations is how we uncover insights about our campaign performance to make them better.

But numbers, charts, and graphs only tell one side of the marketing story. And those who rely solely on them are frequently confused when sales slow or engagement softens.

Don't get me wrong: Data is important, even imperative, when making smart marketing decisions. But this isn't *Moneyball*. We can't base every decision on zeroes and ones. Numbers aren't the ultimate judge of our success.

The ultimate judge of our success is the wildly unpredictable decision making of beautifully complex human beings: our customers.

To be a marketer is to be a student of human behavior. And human beings are not rational decision makers whose choices can be mapped along a neat axis where buyer intent and brand opportunity conveniently intersect. If they were, no one would buy an expensive car. Even if there are differences in cars' maintenance and safety records, some of the highest-rated cars for both are Hyundais and Kias, not Mercedes or BMWs.

Performance marketers may cringe at this, but we cannot call ourselves marketers if we are not more interested in our customers' humanity than in the algorithmic triggers of if-then data decisions.

As we plan, build, and execute our influence marketing campaigns, we have to think about the human qualities not just of our customers and prospective customers but also of our influence partners themselves.

To fail to do so is, to borrow a phrase from Ted Wright from Chapter 14, to treat influential prospects like broadcasters who will simply display our ad. Sure, a certain percentage of their audience will see it, and a smaller percentage may respond or click on it. But bringing their humanity into the equation means more than helping that one ad perform well. It also sows the seeds for future success, because part of being human is building relationships.

In this chapter, I want to share a bit more philosophy with you. You'll hear my perspective on technology and how humans both drive and interact with it. You'll learn more about the flaws in influence marketing software and an approach you can take to account for them. And I'll underline again the focus on relationships in influence marketing.

TECHNOLOGY IS NOT MEANT TO REPLACE HUMANITY

The best marketing is based on consumer research. At the beginning of a marketing cycle or campaign, strategic planners and market researchers survey, conduct focus groups, and pore over thousands of data points looking for that key consumer insight.

A key consumer insight is the critical piece of information the brand needs in order to build a successful cycle or campaign. The reason disruptive technologies like Uber became smash hits isn't just because they were cool. It's because their whole strategy was built around the key consumer insight that if there was technology available (a convenient app) that allowed consumers to summon a ride even from random people, they would prefer that over a taxi most of the time.

The key insight that helped Saturn become one of the biggest automotive success stories of the 1990s was the realization that consumers would rather not buy a car than have to deal with the mind games and haggling of dealing with a salesperson. Saturn offered their cars at "no-haggle" prices: the price on the sticker was the price you paid.

Apple's now legendary Mac vs. PC commercials, officially known as the "Get a Mac" campaign, were driven by the key insight that customer satisfaction rates for Apple computers were far greater than those for PCs, and the laundry list of PC-user complaints were nonexistent in Macs.

All these campaigns used data analysis tools. The best campaigns we see today may even use artificial intelligence, or AI, to crunch the numbers or extrapolate the data and projections. But to date, not a single key consumer insight has been discovered by a computer.

TECHNOLOGY IS ONLY AS GOOD AS ITS USER

You may remember my story about discovering NetBase from the beginning of Chapter 7. That software is classified as a social listening platform. It indexes and analyzes conversations on social networks, blogs, and news sites to report analytics around the conversations.

One of the many data points social listening software delivers is sentiment. Is what was said about the brand or topic positive, negative, or neutral? Most of these software platforms spit out a pie chart with a green wedge for positive conversations, red for negative, and grey for neutral.

For several years, I analyzed and tested most of the top social listening platforms. They each tried to tell me their technology used machine learning to continually improve sentiment scoring. Most promised their sentiment analysis engines were 75, 80, or even 85 percent accurate.

But I never saw a single sentiment report with more than 60 to 65 percent accuracy, compared with the same data scored by humans. And even human analysis produces inconsistencies. If you handed 100 people a slip of paper that said, "I like Ford trucks, but I drive a Toyota Tundra," no more than 80 or 85 of them would agree the statement is positive for both brands. Some of the remaining people would say it's positive for Ford and negative for Toyota. Others would say it is neutral for Toyota.

It's actually a trick question that none of the social listening platforms get right. There's a fourth sentiment category. That sentence is a positive statement for Ford. But it isn't a neutral statement for Toyota. It's undeterminable.

The person said they drove a Toyota Tundra, but they didn't indicate whether they liked it. That's not neutral. Neutral would be, "I drive a Toyota Tundra. It's OK." Leaving out the "OK" part negates our ability to analyze their sentiment toward the Tundra at all.

No algorithm or machine learning process I've seen to date can determine what Toyota can do with that statement. It takes a human being to read the sentence and then understand the context and nuances of the conversation as a whole to discover an insight worth using.

THE INFLUENCE TECHNOLOGY GAP

Influence marketing software is equally flawed. Most influence identification tools are organized around follower counts. You input a topic—let's say landscape design—and the software spits out a list of accounts from various social networks, organized in order from most followers to least. The data is pulled from the social network's API, which allows the software to see and report back on certain data in the social network.

Julius, one of the influence marketing platforms I use frequently, says that on YouTube, the landscape design creator at the top of the pile is Brian's Lawn Maintenance. His channel has about 90,000 subscribers and features equipment reviews, head-to-head challenges with leaf blowers, and the like.

BuzzSumo, another software platform that offers influence analysis, also has Brian's Lawn Maintenance in its database. But it says that CTSCAPER, with 57,000 subscribers, is the top landscape design creator on YouTube.

These two software platforms have access to the same data, yet organize it differently. Yes, I can ask BuzzSumo to change its data organization to focus on subscriber count alone and replicate what Julius shows, but that just proves my point: You have to add human reason and problem solving to the technology to use it appropriately.

Beyond that, however, is the issue that influence software simply gives you data. It does not analyze the content of an potential partner's feed; report back how effective their sponsored content was to their previous brand partners; or tell you how effective they might be in driving their audience to try or buy your product, participate in your promotion, or change their minds about your issue.

All that takes human intervention, analysis, and consideration. Machines can move data from point A to point B. They can present it in different ways. They can run computations and reorganize the data based on parameters you plug in. But they cannot make aesthetic decisions, like whether an influence prospect's attitude, voice, or style fits your brand.

That is up to us humans.

TECHNOLOGY DOESN'T BUILD RELATIONSHIPS

And then there's the ultimate payoff of influence marketing we've discussed previously: Building relationships with your influence partners over time so they become your true partners. That is a human function, not one that takes place in the cloud or on a hard drive.

Yes, technology can be a great help in forming relationships. The vast majority of influence partners I've worked with over the past decade are people I've never been in the same room with. We email, text, FaceTime, Skype, Zoom, Slack, or Hangout. Without the tech, I wouldn't be able to build the relationship as efficiently. But without them or me, the technology wouldn't be able to build it at all.

When you look at programmatic media buying, which is at the other end of the humanity vs. technology spectrum when it comes to marketing, the tech only goes so far. Programmatic media buying is an automated system of buying and placing ads based on computer data analysis. You program in your target audience, budget, etc., and the computers behind all these online engines calculate when and where your ads will run.

Programmatic advertising uses all the data available to it. It can even leverage any user data the person makes available, so ads with relevant things like the user's name can be placed in real time. For example, I get an occasional Facebook ad for genealogy sites saying, "Trace the Falls family back to the 16th century." That's because in my privacy settings, I have allowed Facebook to let advertisers see my name.

Because it is automated, programmatic advertising is almost all technology. There are no human decisions involved other than the inputs the campaign starts with. But when someone clicks on an ad, places an order, or decides to learn more about the product or service, there has to be more than machines at play.

The more human touch that is involved after the click or conversion in programmatic advertising, the more successful the campaign will be. Human consumers are just that—human. They don't want to be treated like a number, a spreadsheet cell, or a data point. They have questions. They want to do business with companies they identify with. They want a good experience. And computers can't handle those things.

Relationships are not ones and zeroes in a database. They're not even driven by rational decision making, so they can't be programmed into code or instructions. They have to be built, managed, and maintained by human beings. The bad news is you can't rely on computer software to solve that problem. The good news is that when it comes to dealing with humans, you already are one.

THE MISTAKE OF TECHNOLOGY

Where technology hurts us as marketers, then, is when we allow it to drive our decision making to the point of ignoring the human aspect of our relationships. It's when we blindly trust the list IZEA or Onalytica spits out without digging into it and analyzing the recommended influence partners' content. It's when we check off the to-do item of having a list of influence partners to leverage, but we forget to see whether they will be effective at persuading their audiences to take action.

Ignoring our human side also happens when we make our "buy" with a given person with influence and overlook the opportunity to make a true value exchange, one that benefits them beyond a paycheck and forges a real relationship with them. If we value making a connection to their audience once, why wouldn't we value it in a deeper, more meaningful way over time?

The answer to that question may depend on your end game. If you're trying to sell those last few units of a product before you go out of business or sell your company to a larger corporation and disappear to Tahiti forever, maybe you don't care about the long game. But 99.9 percent of the time, you do. Or you should.

Relying only on technology to achieve your goals is a grave mistake made by short-timers and posers. Instead, let's embrace the technology for the value it adds. Influence marketing software helps feed us information, organizes it so we can apply our own thinking to it, and assists us in making good decisions. Communications technology empowers us to connect with our influence partners in dozens of ways to build our relationship with them, providing value for them while they do the same for us.

Think of the technology as the automobile, and you as the driver. You set the destination. Even a self-driving car doesn't just take you to random places—you have to tell it where to go. If you don't, it doesn't go anywhere.

Removing the human element from your influence marketing produces similar results.

17

BECOMING AN INFLUENTIAL BRAND

B y now, hopefully, it should be clear that this book isn't about becoming a person of influence yourself. There are dozens of titles out there about how to become big on Instagram or build an incredible YouTube following. This book, thus far, has focused on how to think about influence in a larger context for your business: how to Winfluence.

However, there is great opportunity not just in leveraging influence partners to communicate with consumers, but also in your business becoming an influential voice in its own right. Theoretically, if people in your marketplace listen when you talk, you've got all the influence you need.

Thus one goal of your brand's approach to influence marketing should be to establish your own influence. What have we defined as the qualities an influential person has that make them influential? Their audience knows them, likes them, and trusts them. You must then do things that produce those reactions to your brand.

Generally, this involves thought leadership. Sometimes it is the byproduct of having great products or services. And other times it is the result of leveraging the influence of others to associate your brand with their know/like/trust qualities.

This chapter explains the steps your brand must take to become an influential voice in its own right. I'll show you how individual companies have succeeded in creating their own sphere of influence. And you'll learn how to do it yourself by building trust with your audience through compelling content and engagement.

BECOMING A THOUGHT LEADER

HubSpot (hubspot.com) is perhaps the best example of a B2B company leveraging influence marketing for advertising, even though they might argue it's not advertising at all. The "inbound marketing" company sells software that does everything from hosting a business's website to fueling its own lead-generation and CRM sales functions, managing its social media networks, handling email marketing, and more.

The company, founded in 2006 by Dharmesh Shah and Brian Halligan, preaches the gospel of inbound marketing—creating content that attracts customers to you, rather than the old method of going to them through advertising. It became an influential company in the marketing software space by first creating software to power an inbound marketing engine and then teaching potential customers about the power of inbound marketing.

The concept of inbound marketing is predicated on know/like/trust principles. Your brand creates content that is useful to your target audience. You promote that content to ensure that audience has an opportunity to consume it. (Yes, there's still some traditional advertising tactics in the mix.) In order for them to consume the content, however, they have to give you contact information, which generates a new lead in your marketing funnel.

At that point, you can either sell to them (not recommended) or continue to feed them more opportunities to consume different useful content, building their trust in you over time. They now know you. As they get smarter about the topics you are an authority on, they like you. Eventually, you become the place they go to for knowledge. They trust you.

HubSpot eventually became an authority on becoming an authority. And the software they sell is one mechanism you can use to power yourself into becoming an authority.

That brilliance helped HubSpot explode from a small Boston startup in 2006 to a $759 million valuation at its IPO just eight years later.

To be fair, HubSpot didn't grow that big that fast by just practicing inbound marketing. When I visited the company headquarters in 2013, I walked through a room with probably 100 or more telephone sales representatives, who undoubtedly were not all taking inbound calls. But the philosophy behind inbound marketing does create influence. And it does it just like your favorite online influencer.

THE INFLUENCE APPROACH TO BUILDING TRUST

At the core of any online influencer's brand, you will find content. If they don't have content, there's nothing for an audience to see, so no audience accumulates. Some produce image-heavy content conveying their sense of style, beauty, fashion, or art. People come to know, like, and trust that creator for inspiration, ideas, or perhaps advice.

Others produce engaging video content for YouTube or Facebook Live or TikTok. The audience enjoys their take on the topics they cover, the entertainment value of the conversations they have, the interviews they conduct, or the silly stunts they record. Users of those networks come to know, like, and trust them for the entertainment or information—or both—in their videos.

Some find and share interesting content on Twitter, becoming great curators for their audience. They may also engage their audience in real-time conversations on a given subject matter and provide their own expertise and opinions, 280 characters at a time. Eventually, an audience follows the know/like/trust path, and the creator can have an impact on their followers.

Others produce written content in the form of articles they post on a blog or online news site, where the audience dives in and develops a know/like/trust continuum based on the influential author's expertise. They become a sort of media outlet for the audience, and as their audience grows, they also become an influential voice in their main topic.

Many of these online influencers combine multiple channels of content—a blog, YouTube channel, Instagram feed, Facebook page, Twitter presence, etc.—to diversify their sphere of influence and grow their audience in multiple ways. This is smart because not every channel is as effective for certain types of authority.

How-to content is very effective on YouTube, but it doesn't translate well on Twitter if it involves a lot of steps. But the person who produced the great how-to video on YouTube can be incredibly useful answering questions about the topic in a real-time Twitter chat.

Now, in your mind's eye, remove the online influencer from the equation and replace them with your brand.

Imagine your brand is creating the engaging how-to videos on YouTube. Then it hosts a Twitter chat to answer questions from consumers about the topic. It produces a longer, written piece for the company's online magazine and shares success story images of finished how-tos on Instagram to inspire others.

Any brand can do this. The only change from what most brands do online is in the purpose and approach. The purpose is to create know/like/trust conversions in the online audience. That happens through producing great content that attracts an audience.

Remember, the purpose is not selling your product or service. That will happen. But you first have to create a reason for people to know you—the content. You have to then give them a reason to like you—by making the content useful. Then you must earn their trust—by giving them useful content over time.

Along the way, you can suggest they buy your product or service to help them complete the recommended tasks. You can even have your own "sponsored" content where you dive deep into a product's features or benefits, convincing them your product is the best one to buy for this type of work or project.

TeamValvoline (team.valvoline.com) is a content hub for Valvoline Inc. There you can find articles about how to fix and care for cars, but also content around auto racing, niche automotive interests like vanning, and more. Cornett created TeamValvoline with the brand in 2015.

One article I found there was about the challenges of caring for hybrid cars. It was written by an editor from *Popular Mechanics*, who contributed the piece just like a journalist would for a magazine's website. It wasn't specifically about buying oil for hybrid cars, though the writer quoted a technology manager at Valvoline in the story. (You can see the article at https://team.valvoline.com/diy/product-tools/valvolines-answer-unique-challenges-hybrid-cars.)

TeamValvoline is a branded environment, so there are plenty of product-centric spaces there. There are images of Valvoline products in the articles but no real advertisements. The content hub is built to attract audiences interested in automotive topics. Once they know it's there, they come and consume useful content to help them care for their vehicles or entertain or inspire them about fast cars and high-performance engines. They like the content and the brand for providing it. Over time, they come to trust TeamValvoline and the Valvoline brand as a resource for this education and entertainment.

TeamValvoline is a brand with influence. And it is a content product of an oil company.

THE INFLUENCE BRAND LESSON FROM THE CONTENT MARKETING MASTERS

While TeamValvoline is obviously branded, other influential brand platforms are more subtle. *Home Made Simple* may be one of the most influential platforms among women in the U.S. today. The weekly TV program hosted by Laila Ali is in its ninth season on the Oprah Winfrey Network. But before it was a TV show, *Home Made Simple* was a website. Or, more accurately, a blog.

Home Made Simple (homemadesimple.com) launched in 2000 as a microsite extension of Women.com. The site still earns 30,000 visitors per month, according to SEMrush, but at various times through the years, it has been one of the highest-trafficked how-to sites for content that appeals to homemakers. Before it became a TV show, Home Made Simple even published a book with St. Martin's Press in 2010 called *Home Made Simple: Fresh Ideas to Make Your Own*. It recently launched a line of branded products, too.

With a popular site, a book, and a TV show, it is a mega brand among women.

Except that it's not a brand. Since 2001, the website and all its various offshoots have been a fully funded extension of Procter & Gamble. It is a brand publishing platform.

"Home Made Simple was the result of a joint brainstorming session with our team and the fabric and home care brand management team," explained Lillian Gilden, then the vice president of the strategic alliance team at Women.com. "We developed and launched a microsite and newsletter for the sponsoring brands in response to Procter & Gamble's RFP."

The site was a collaboration of four sponsoring brands—Febreze, Cascade, Dawn, and Swiffer. Those continue to be the core underwriters of the site and subsequent extensions of the Home Made Simple platform.

And they're not trying to hide it. Procter & Gamble has always fully disclosed its involvement. But they positioned it as a useful resource for advice and ideas around housecleaning, craft projects, style, and design. P&G products have always been props and background material, conveniently placed where opportunity allowed, but the focus was on delivering great content.

This is a 21st-century application of what Procter & Gamble has long known: Content is the best way to attract an audience. That was the strategy behind the company's original foray into content marketing when it created the soap opera on radio in the 1920s. Those became the holy grail of influence. Housewives everywhere were locked into their radio dramas in the afternoons. Since Tide was paying for the production, it was the soap that brought them their operas.

But ultimately what Procter & Gamble has been doing for almost 100 years now is creating influence over an audience, then leveraging that influence for their brands.

THE B2B TWITTER VERSION OF BECOMING AN INFLUENTIAL BRAND

Marc Meyer looked at his client's Twitter account one day and basically thought, "Meh." The B2B technology company's account was seeing 100,000 to 150,000 impressions per month. They were sharing content, linking to articles, adding images, using hashtags—all the things the "experts" said a business should do on social media. The impressions were strong for a company in that industry.

But the engagement rate was about 0.05 percent. That's one like, comment, or share for every 2,000 impressions.

"I started looking at the effectiveness of our stuff vs. others and started paying attention to what the 'influencers' did and who they did it with," Meyer explained. "And I started noticing some trends."

Meyer saw how influential creators continually feed off each other as much as others try to feed off of them. He studied and charted the types of content they were pushing, whose content it was, and whom they were directing it toward.

He came up with a list. Successful influence content:

* Was very visual in nature (images, videos)
* Used a lot of hashtags
* Tagged and included other influential creators in the post
* Had no regard for time of day or frequency—Twitter is on 24/7 and nonstop
* Frequently used third-party content, but didn't always attribute it properly

Meyer shifted the company's content to mirror the successful habits of notable industry creators. He tossed the 9 to 5 work-hour limitations on posting and began scheduling content every two hours. He incorporated third-party content 75 percent of the time. He frequently tagged all the major industry influence holders in posts and added up to ten hashtags per post based on the topic.

"The results were crazy," he said. "We went from having zero influencers following us to all of them following us. Our impressions went from 100,000 per month to over a million. Our engagement rate went from 0.05 percent to anywhere from 4 to 9 percent."

In other words, Meyer shifted the company's social media account to act more like an online influencer. Guess what happened? The company became one.

Onalytica rated the company as the No. 41 most influential "person" in their industry after the change. A different rating I found of blogs and websites in their vertical listed them as the No. 6 resource in the industry behind industry magazines and two mega-brand content platforms.

Followers on Twitter grew by a factor of ten. Leads multiplied by three and conversions by five.

"It was startling," Meyer said.

Perhaps more jolting is the fact that 100 percent of the change was organic. It was just a smart guy playing out a hunch and shifting the way a brand behaved on social media to be more like the influential people around it.

What Meyer did with his client on Twitter is just a 280-character, B2B version of P&G's soap operas. Create the type of content people are engaged with. Then, while being careful not to abuse the privilege of their attention, you smartly build and/or present them with awareness of, or even calls to action for, your product.

IS IT INFLUENCE MARKETING OR CONTENT MARKETING?

Home Made Simple and soap operas have always been claimed by content marketers as their gold standards. And they're right. It's a strategic use of content to attract an audience. But without content, it's hard to earn influence.

Quick! Think of someone with influence who doesn't produce content.

Political leaders have great influence but may not have big online followings. Still, they produce very important content in the form of government policies, campaign platforms, and laws. Members of the clergy are also incredibly influential, but they produce sermons and other educational materials in line with their faith to shepherd their congregations.

Until 2007, you could argue that the Kardashians didn't have influence. At least not the kind they have now. But they also didn't have a TV show or Instagram channels before then.

(Yes, I understand some people think the Kardashians still don't produce anything that qualifies as content, but this is a book, not a comedy club.)

It takes content to produce influence. If your brand is not in the content marketing game, producing blog posts, videos, social media content, webinars, white papers, or apps, then you are relegated to leveraging other people's influence to reach audiences.

That may mean paying a TV network to leverage the influence it has earned by building great content to attract viewers and infrastructure to produce reach across a population. It may also mean you build a relationship with a 22-year-old who takes pictures of her food and posts them on Instagram because 400,000 people love looking at her dinner.

In the happy middle are brands that do both. They produce useful, compelling, and engaging content that serves their current or prospective customers in a way that moves them from knowing to liking to trusting them. They present those customers with opportunities to both buy and engage with the brand along the way. And they ultimately create long-term relationships where those customers buy and buy again.

But they also build relationships with influential people, both online and off-line, who gain value from knowing them and provide value by giving access to their sphere of influence—their audience. They may partner with people of influence to create content, share the brand's content with their audience, or tell their audience about the brand's product, services, events, or ideas in their own original way.

Those influence partners may be Instagrammers or they may be city council members. They may have massive YouTube followings, or they may have just a few hundred of the right followers on a given network. They may be recommended by a big influence marketing software search result, or they may be a lobbyist who can get closed-door meetings with state representatives in the capitol.

All marketing is about influence. You're trying to influence the way people think about a product, service, or issue. You're trying to influence buying preferences or public opinions. People who have built online networks of influence are important here. But so are people who don't have the time to cultivate their follower counts or likes, preferring to build influence over people in less virtual worlds.

When you sit down to plan your next marketing campaign, remember you're ultimately trying to influence a group of people to do something or think something. The approach to building strategies and tactics and executing them to achieve that which I've spelled out in this book should serve as a useful guide.

And if you follow the recommendations in these pages, you won't just produce influence marketing campaigns. You won't just influence. You'll Winfluence.

WINFLUENCE PRIORITY SCORECARD

As mentioned in Chapter 15, the following is a Winfluence Priortity Scorecard for your use.

☐ WINFLUENCE PRIORITY SCORECARD ☐

GOAL: ☐ SALES   ☐ BRAND AWARENESS   **SCALE:** ☐ GLOBAL ☐ NATIONAL ☐ REGIONAL ☐ LOCAL
☐ CONVERSIONS ☐ FOLLOWERS
☐ TRAFFIC   ☐ PERCEPTION CHANGE   **INFLUENCER:** _____   **NETWORKS:** ☐ FACEBOOK ☐ TWITTER ☐ PINTEREST
☐ INSTAGRAM ☐ LINKEDIN ☐ YOUTUBE
☐ TIKTOK ☐ OTHER ☐ OFFLINE

REACH

- IMPRESSIONS   [ ] SCORE 1-10
- LIKES   [ ] SCORE 1-10
- COMMENTS   [ ] SCORE 1-10
- SHARES   [ ] SCORE 1-10

RELEVANCE

- TOPIC ALIGNMENT   [ ] SCORE 1-10
- BRAND ALIGNMENT   [ ] SCORE 1-10
- COMMENTS   [ ] SCORE 1-10
- SHARES   [ ] SCORE 1-10

RESONANCE

- AUTHORITY   [ ] SCORE 1-10
- IMPACT   [ ] SCORE 1-10
- SHARES   [ ] SCORE 1-10

TOTAL REACH [ ] + TOTAL RELEVANCE [ ] + TOTAL RESONANCE [ ] = [ ] WINFLUENCE QUALITY SCORE

B

WINFLUENCE SUCCESS SCORECARD

Also mentioned in Chapter 15, is the Winfluence Success Scorecard. The following is one for your personal use.

□ WINFLUENCE SUCCESS SCORECARD □

PROJECT/CAMPAIGN _____ DATES ACTIVE _____ BRAND/PRODUCT _____

PRIMARY GOAL: □ SALES □ CONVERSIONS □ TRAFFIC □ AWARENESS □ PERCEPTION □ OTHER _____

SALES [* TOTALS FROM INFLUENCER CHANNELS ONLY (PREFERRED)]

UNITS SOLD* _____

GROSS REVENUE* _____ ROI _____ (GROSS REV-COST/COST)

INFLUENCER PLACEMENTS _____ CPP _____

IMPRESSIONS _____ CPI _____

VIEWS (IF APPLICABLE) _____ CPV _____

ENGAGEMENTS _____ CPE _____

COST _____

AWARENESS

% AWARE (PRE) _____ % AWARE (POST) _____

PCT. CHANGE _____

ONLINE MENTIONS (PRE) _____ (POST) _____

PCT. CHANGE _____

FOLLOWER COUNT (PRE) _____ (POST) _____

PCT. CHANGE _____

INFLUENCER PLACEMENTS _____ CPP _____

IMPRESSIONS _____ CPI _____

VIEWS (IF APPLICABLE) _____ CPV _____

ENGAGEMENTS _____ CPE _____

COST _____

CONVERSIONS [* TOTALS FROM INFLUENCER CHANNELS ONLY (PREFERRED)]

CONVERSIONS* _____ COST PER _____

CONVERSION VALUE _____ ROI _____ (CONV.VALUE-COST)/COST

INFLUENCER PLACEMENTS _____ CPP _____

IMPRESSIONS _____ CPI _____

VIEWS (IF APPLICABLE) _____ CPV _____

ENGAGEMENTS _____ CPE _____

COST _____

PERCEPTION

% TRUE (PRE) _____ % TRUE (POST) _____

PCT. CHANGE _____

ONLINE MENTIONS (PRE) _____ (POST) _____

PCT. CHANGE _____

INFLUENCER PLACEMENTS _____ CPP _____

IMPRESSIONS _____ CPI _____

VIEWS (IF APPLICABLE) _____ CPV _____

ENGAGEMENTS _____ CPE _____

COST _____

TRAFFIC

SITE USERS _____ CPV _____

CONVERSIONS/UNITS SOLD _____

CONVERSION VALUE*/ _____ ROI _____

GROSS REVENUE

INFLUENCER PLACEMENTS _____ CPP _____

IMPRESSIONS _____ CPI _____

VIEWS (IF APPLICABLE) _____ CPV _____

ENGAGEMENTS _____ CPE _____

COST _____

OTHER

1. _____

2. _____

3. _____

4. _____

5. _____

6. _____

7. _____

8. _____

COST _____

ACKNOWLEDGMENTS

There's a good chance if you think I should be thanking you for contributing to this book in some way, you're probably right. So thank you. Truly.

Acknowledgments are hard because you always end up leaving someone out who probably should have been in there. I can go back to childhood and thank my parents, family, teachers, friends, professors, bosses, colleagues, clients, priests, pastors, and therapists, not to mention the dozens of people at Entrepreneur Press who actually made the real book (or the electronic version) you hold in your hands, and I would still miss some people.

And let's face it, the only people who actually read the acknowledgments are the ones who think they might be mentioned. So again . . . thank YOU. For that thing you said or did, or that role you played. It was important. It meant something. It helped. I appreciate you.

Erik Deckers dragged me into this book writing mess a decade ago, and I'm glad he did. Some combination of my mother, my high school English teachers, and probably Dave Barry taught me how to write, so they deserve some credit. Gary Krebs called me out of the blue last year and said, "It's high time you wrote another book." He was right and became my first real agent, which is significant in that I can now say I have an agent. It's not as fancy as you might think, but it does sound fancy.

All the people quoted and mentioned in this book had a lot to do with it successfully coming together. Tiffany Mitchell and Ted Wright bent over backward to help make their parts really good. Sarah Clevenger's illustrations brought it to life. She keeps thanking me for the opportunity, but all the thank-yous should be from me. And if you had told me ten years ago THE David Meerman Scott would one day write a foreword to a book of mine, I would have sworn someone had slipped me a mickey. Thank you, David.

I was tickled when Entrepreneur Press bought the book because I've worked with them since Amy Cosper's days at the magazine and have always felt valued by their team. That's a big deal even if you don't have a fragile ego. Super big thanks to Jennifer Dorsey, Karen Billipp, Wyn Hilty, and the rest of the team for allowing me to argue my points . . . and sometimes letting me win.

My team at Cornett has been incredibly supportive, constantly cheering me on with this project. Kip Cornett, Christy Hiler, and crew invited a loud-mouthed, egotistical bastard to come work with them. I've never been happier at an agency. Especially the day Matt Hudgins observed that I am steeped with "curmudgeon energy."

I have to call out my influence marketing partner in crime, Allen Marler. He actually creates and manages many of Cornett's influence marketing projects, a few of which are detailed in these pages. He could have written this book himself and will probably outdo me with his own one day. Madison Moynihan also deserves credit and recognition. She makes a lot of our influence marketing and social media programs run so well that you sometimes forget someone had to do all that work.

The rest of the Cornett team is a godsend. Thank you all for the encouragement, support, and collaboration.

You don't get to tell great stories about influence marketing without great clients and influence relationships. We've got some amazing ones at Cornett, and I've had the honor of working with many other good ones over the years. Thank all of you for letting me be a part of your brands and experiences.

And since I'm not a full-time writer, all this work happened with the tolerance and support, if not permission, of my family. Of course, Grant and Katie, my teenage kids, would rather Snapchat or Instagram than talk to me, so they didn't mind much. But they did give me the space to write and the love and support I need to be able to give the same right back to them.

Their mother, Nancy, continues to be a great partner in co-parenting and a support system in ways she thought she wouldn't have to be anymore. I can't thank her enough for that.

Without Julie Moore, I wouldn't have much sanity. She has been a tremendous encourager, filter, intellectual sparring partner, and motivator. I'm so very thankful we found each other and love again.

Julie's kids, Gus and Kate, may not be great at being quiet while I'm trying to write, but they sure are awesome at making a guy feel loved and supported. They don't have to like their mom's boyfriend, but they do. And I'm grateful for that.

Thank you to my mother for being my number-one fan, advocate, and sounding board. I'm glad I finally grew up enough to be hers, too. To my step-father, Gary George, for raising me to have a strong work ethic. And thanks to my dad for my sick sense of humor. (And to Mom for adding enough filter and decorum to make me somewhat less of a nuisance.)

Finally, I have to thank Katherine Bull. She was my first editor. She made me an author. I only wish she were still around to see this. Rest in peace, sweet lady.

—Jason Falls, Summer 2020

ABOUT THE AUTHOR

Jason Falls solves problems. Most of the time they have to do with digital marketing for Cornett, a full-service advertising agency based in Lexington, Kentucky, where he leads digital strategy. His work has touched a number of major brands and has been recognized with several national and many regional awards, including a 2019 Shorty Award for his influence marketing work.

A public relations professional by trade and writer by craft, Falls has co-written two other books—*No Bullshit Social Media: The All-Business, No-Hype Guide to Social Media Marketing* (Que 2011) and *The Rebel's Guide to Email Marketing: Grow Your List, Break the Rules, and Win* (Que 2012). Falls is also an innovator in the social analytics space, having published the first-ever research report on online conversations in 2012. Noted as influential in the social technology and marketing space by *Entrepreneur*, *Advertising Age*, and others, Falls is a frequent media analyst and guest, appearing on or in outlets like the BBC World Service, ESPN's *Outside the Lines*, *The Wall Street Journal*, *USA Today*, *Bloomberg Businessweek*, *Forbes*, and NPR.

Falls hosts two podcasts: *Digging Deeper—Make Creativity Your Business Advantage*, which features weekly interviews focused on marketing creativity, and *Winfluence—The Influence Marketing Podcast*, which is a companion to this book. You can find links to both at winfluencebook.com.

He and his two children live in Louisville, Kentucky.

About the Illustrator

All inside illustrations for Winfluence are by visual artist Sarah Clevenger. Also based in Louisville, Kentucky, Clevenger is best known for her mixed-media paintings combining ink, watercolor, and gold leaf to bring out vibrant, engaging colors in a unique style. By day, however, she is a social media strategy consultant with considerable experience in the health-care and wellness space. She also served with Jason Falls on the Louisville Digital Association's board of directors for several years. Find more of her work at sarahclevengerart.com.

INDEX

CPSIA information can be obtained
at www.ICGtesting.com
Printed in the USA
LVHW030123120121
676136LV00005B/5